* * * * * * *

Harrison

* * * * * * *

FOREWORD BY

Olivia Harrison

INTRODUCTION BY

Jann S. Wenner

EDITED BY

Jason Fine

SIMON AND SCHUSTER

NEW YORK   LONDON   TORONTO   SYDNEY   SINGAPORE

Harrison

BY THE

EDITORS OF

Rolling Stone

EDITOR: Robert Love
EXECUTIVE EDITOR: Jason Fine
ASSOCIATE EDITOR: Jenny Eliscu

DESIGNERS: Gail Anderson, Siung Tjia, Ken DeLago
DESIGN ASSOCIATE: Jessica Disbrow
PHOTOGRAPHY EDITOR: Audrey Landreth
ASSOCIATE PHOTOGRAPHY EDITOR: Tara Canova

PROJECT COORDINATOR: Nina Pearlman
COPY EDITOR: Robin Aigner
RESEARCH: Jason Stutts
BUSINESS MANAGER: Evelyn Bernal

SIMON & SCHUSTER
Rockefeller Center
1230 Avenue of the Americas
New York, NY 10020

Manufactured in the United States of America

10 9 8 7 6 5 4 3 2 1

Library of Congress Cataloging-in-Publication
Data is available.
ISBN 0-7432-3581-9

Portions of this book originally appeared in
ROLLING STONE

For information regarding special discounts
for bulk purchases, please contact Simon & Schuster
Special Sales at 1-800-456-6798
or business@simonandschuster.com

TABLE OF CONTENTS

A Few Words About George

BY OLIVIA HARRISON

✦ ✦ ⋒ ✦ ✦

THE SILENCE of George's absence in our lives is deafening. Although he often renounced his role as an entertainer, my life with him was never boring. There were many comedies and a few tragedies but, most of all, deep love for all living things. He was a warrior who faced life's battles with extraordinary courage. In the words of Bob Dylan, "He had the strength of a hundred men." The power of his convictions was as strong as a hundred men, all right. As Arjuna asked Krishna for guidance on the battlefield, so George faced the many battles before him with spiritual courage and unwavering conviction.

Our son, Dhani, and I, like George's friends, were spoiled by his rich and loving presence: from the morning wake-up call, which could have been (depending on our location and mood) a morning raga, a Vedic chant, a Mozart concerto, Cab Calloway's "Bugle Call Rag," or Hoagy's earliest instrumental version of "Stardust," to the day's final tune, maybe whistled on his way to bed and which I would wake up in the morning singing. He loved

planting the seed of a song and would sometimes whistle a tune I disliked just to see if he could get it rolling around in my head. After I would complain about it, he'd say, "Okay, here's one to replace it," and whistle another.

All senses were satisfied as incense blew in the morning breeze, mingling with the steam from hot cups of tea. If he stepped out the door for a breath of morning air, he always returned with a flower or leaf that would have gone unnoticed by everyone else, in the same way many among us would have gone unnoticed were it not for his ability to "see" the true person inside the bodily form. He always went straight to the heart of a person, and that ability extended to any subject or matter or work before him. His ability to penetrate to the core gave him, as he put it, "a different slant, a different patter," than anyone I ever knew.

George said he felt closest to God in nature, and some may assume his passion as a landscape gardener was founded solely on his immense love and knowledge of plants as well as his extraordinary vision. But the driving force was his desire to know God. "If there is a God, we must see Him; if there is a soul we must perceive it. Otherwise it is better not to believe. It is better to be an outspoken atheist than a hypocrite," as he used to remind us! Though he often quoted spiritual greats in this way, George did not, contrary to popular belief, "belong" to any spiritual organization, although many claimed him as their own. George also said, "He who tells *all* that he knows, tells *more* than he knows." This usually applied to those who declared they knew the very private George's innermost beliefs. In fact, his spiritual knowledge and experience was many faceted. Still, he managed to dive deep to the heart of each practice, never content to skim the surface. He embraced the *essence* of all religions although he had little patience for organized religions or dogma that espoused guilt, sin or mystery. For George, there was no mystery, and he would gladly spend hours discussing God with an interested person—and some not so interested!

He was so deep, and I for one was at times guilty of indolence—probably because I knew that the tide of his devotion was so strong that I could ride those currents with him toward our shared goal of God consciousness. Now, without him, we all have more paddling to do.

George left the world his uniquely beautiful melodies, and some of them were barely born, played once, maybe. Every Dictaphone or tape machine in the house was found with a cassette inside bearing the beginning of a new song, some on piano, ukulele or guitar, some with hysterically funny words, some with fiercely serious lyrics, but all crafted from creativity he knew to be a divine gift.

Besides the company, conversation and wisdom of my beloved friend, I already long for the live background music to our lives. If I began singing a song—any song—he would accompany and encourage me. If I played three chords on the uke (compulsory instrument in our home), he would be my band. George was so generous and "grateful to anyone that is happy or free." A good moment to him was always worth making better.

I love you, George. The joys, sorrows, lessons and love we shared are more than enough to fill my heart until we meet again.

—January 2002

We'll Meet Again

"**B**EWARE OF SADNESS**,**" George Harrison sang in one of his most beautiful ballads. "It can hit you, it can hurt you/Make you sore, and what is more/That is not what you are here for." In that spirit, ROLLING STONE created this book, to honor one of rock & roll's greatest heroes for his joyful life, his searching music, and his deep and enduring spirit.

Harrison contains more than one hundred photos from throughout his career, as well as new essays and material drawn from more than thirty years of ROLLING STONE's coverage. Particularly moving are the remembrances of the former Beatle by the artists who knew him best, including Bob Dylan, Tom Petty, Mick Jagger, Keith Richards, Paul Simon, Elton John, Yoko Ono and Jim Keltner. In their fond reminiscences, those musicians perfectly set the tone of this book. They are, of course, saddened by the untimely death of their friend. But they insist on celebrating his music and his life—the beauty, the spiritual ambition, the struggle, the achievement, the inspiration. So we join those voices as a chorus, offering this commemorative book as a gift from one small group of Harrison's fans to the many others, an acknowledgment of why he means so much to us.

Harrison, first of all, was a wonderful musician, a guitarist who was never showy but who had an innate, eloquent melodic sense. He played exquisitely in the service of the song, whether it was one of his own, one written by John Lennon or Paul McCartney, or, as in the Beatles' early days, one by his heroes Carl Perkins and Chuck Berry. His ability to craft a unique approach to every song is one important reason that the Beatles' work has sounded fresh year after year, generation after generation. Sometimes overlooked because of the subtlety of his style, he has exerted an enormous influence on other musicians.

Beyond that, Harrison was a first-rate songwriter. As all great soul music does, his most beautiful songs–"Something," "My Sweet Lord," "While My Guitar Gently Weeps"–blended human and divine love. Because he did not have great range as a singer, his voice took on a yearning quality that perfectly expressed the way his songs reached for a state of bliss that seemed just beyond earthly reach. He seemed always to be aspiring, searching for a state of perfection. And, happily, Harrison's spirituality was not just a matter of locating an "inner light," as he once put it. It meant acting in the world to relieve suffering, as his work organizing the Concert for Bangladesh and the Romanian Angel Appeal demonstrated.

Harrison had a sense of humor, too. His production company, HandMade Films, got its start when his Monty Python buddies couldn't raise the money for *Life of Brian,* a parody of the life of Christ, and he stepped in with the cash. And when he spoke about his years with the Beatles, he would often begin anecdotes with "It was just like the Rutles" or would affectionately dismiss the group as "the Fabs."

"If you can't feel the spirit of some friend who's been that close," Harrison said about Lennon after he died, "then what chance have you got of feeling the spirit of Christ or Buddha or whoever else you may be interested in? 'If your memory serves you well, we're going to meet again.' I believe that."

As well as a proclamation of faith, that statement was a challenge: It is essential human work to keep the spirit of the people you love alive within yourself. We can feel George Harrison within these pages, and we hope that you will, too.

–JANN S. WENNER

The
MYSTERY
Inside

George

By Mikal Gilmore

EORGE HIMSELF is no mystery," John Lennon said in 1968. "But the mystery inside George is immense. It's watching him uncover it all little by little that's so damn interesting." George Harrison was, in the early days of the Beatles' fame, the most unknowable personality of this sudden, inexorable force that was changing culture and history—and then later he seemed the band's most forward-looking and surprising hidden treasure. When the Beatles ended, Harrison initially reaped the greatest solo successes. He made a masterful and loving epic post-Beatle solo work and followed it with the most singular concert in

Harrison, at thirteen, with his first guitar (a secondhand acoustic), now on display at the Rock & Roll Hall of Fame

rock & roll's history. But since the mid-1970s, Harrison had receded from public view and from the popular-music arena, into the massive confines of his mansion outside London, into carefully shielded seclusion, into reported fears, into a deliberate distance from contemporary pop vogues.

"Being a Beatle was a nightmare," Harrison once said. "A horror story. I don't even like to think about it." The Beatles received an extraordinary bounty of love in their career and lives—and each of them told the world through their music that love was the key act of faith and will that could save us. How, then, did such gifts and such an outlook translate into a nightmare for the gift-givers? The person who could have answered that question died on November 29, 2001, after a brave and dignified battle with not just death but with life.

A Harrison family portrait, 1951: George (center), surrounded by (from left) father Harry, older brothers Harry and Peter, and mother Louise

EORGE HARRISON sometimes referred to himself and Ringo Starr as "economy-class Beatles." In a way, it was a remark that was both self-deprecating and barbed—a way of pointing out that Paul McCartney and John Lennon were the acknowledged and envied creative center at the heart of the world's most beloved rock & roll band, not to mention its wealthiest members. By contrast, he and Starr were seen as gifted yet lucky accompanists. But there was something revealing in the comment about the Beatles' historic and class origins. Years ago it was possible to visit Liverpool and see the homes and districts where the group's members grew up, before these areas were cleaned up a bit for tourist traffic and declared official

birthplaces. What one discovered from such a visit was eye-opening: John Lennon—the Beatle who most passionately promoted his working-class sympathies and identity—grew up in relative comfort compared to his band mates. The others—especially Harrison and Starr—grew up in tougher, riskier, more run-down areas that would, by American standards, be considered low-income housing projects.

Apparently, though, Harrison didn't feel especially deprived in his childhood. Indeed, of all the Beatles, he probably grew up in the home that provided the greatest sense of continuity and support. His father, Harold Harrison, came from working-class Liverpool lineage. At age fourteen, Harry was already supporting himself, and by his seventeenth year, he was a steward aboard a famed ocean liner. In May 1930, Harry married Louise French. By the time Harry was ready to settle ashore in Liverpool with his wife in 1936, the Depression that had gripped America had spread to England and Europe and it hit Liverpool hard. For more than a year, Harry and Louise had to live on the dole–like many other proud Liverpudlians.

Harry eventually took work as a bus driver, and the family settled into a Liverpool working-class suburb. In 1931, the Harrisons' first child, Louise–named after her mother–was born. In 1934, the family gave birth to its first son, Harry, and in 1940 (the same year that John Lennon was born), the Harrisons had a second son, Peter. In those days Goering's Luftwaffe was making bombing raids over the city, destroying Liverpool's famed docks. The town's citizens were living with fear and endangerment as a daily reality, and they were also living with rationed food supplies and a sense of economic limitations that–war or no war–continued to set parts of England's north apart from the wealthier areas of its south. It was in these circumstances that Harrison (named after King George VI) was born on February 25, 1943, as the family's unexpected final addition. The family was strained economically during this period, and in 1949, the Harrisons moved to a council house in Speke–a nearby district known as a poor and tough area.

Later, Harrison would describe Liverpool and its surrounding environs at that time as being like New York City's Bowery. Even so, the Harrisons seemed a tight family (George's mother described her youngest son as "seldom misbehaved . . . bright . . . and extremely independent"). Harry Sr. was seen as a stern but fair man (he prided himself on being Liverpool's best bus operator and later became a top union official for the city's drivers), and Louise enjoyed the reputation of a generous and convivial woman but was also somebody who, like George, had little patience for abiding people who imposed on her. In any event, the family wasn't terribly ambitious in its hopes–which was typical of Liverpudlians in the aftermath of the war. The older sons, Harry and Peter, quit school early on. George ended up as the family's only boy who made it through grammar school and, in 1954, into high school. By all accounts, including his own, he was not a distinguished or reverent student–though, like many young people in England and America at that time, his lack of interest in conventional academic and social standards was more an affirmation of his wits than it was a sign of any lack of

them. That's because George Harrison–like the other young men with whom he would soon form a famous bond–was witnessing the birth of a social and cultural upheaval that became known as rock & roll: the clamor of young people, kicking hard against the 1950s ethos of repression. In many ways, Britain was as ripe for a pop cataclysm as America had been for Elvis Presley in the ennui following world war. In England–catching the reverberations of not just Presley, but the jazz milieu of Miles Davis and Jack Kerouac–the youth scene would acquire the status of a mammoth subcultural class: the byproduct of a postwar population, top-heavy with people under the age of eighteen. For those people, pop music signified the idea of autonomous society. British teenagers weren't just rejecting their parents' values, they were superseding them, though they were also acting out their eminence in American terms–in the music of Presley and rockabilly, in blues and jazz tradition.

Liverpool, more than most British cities, was ripe for the rock & roll explosion. American sailors were regular visitors to the city because of its naval stockyards, and–like German tourists who also occasionally came through the town–these visitors sometimes brought the latest R&B and dance singles, and Liverpool's record stores were prone to stocking fresh American sounds that were either too rough or too new to have yet made an appearance on BBC radio. By the time he was thirteen Harrison was caught up in the new rock & roll, rockabilly and country sounds. In particular, he was enamored of the Sun recordings of Carl Perkins and Elvis Presley, and he thought Little Richard was wild beyond belief. At this time, British school boys were expected to dress in neat clothes or in young men's suits, but Harrison took to wearing skintight pants and greased-back hair, in the manner of other teddy boys–the British youth contingent that adopted American rockabilly as a cause and that was seen as the U.K.'s equivalent of juvenile delinquents. When Harry Sr. expressed concern about this rebellious appearance, George's mother supported her youngest son's boldness. "There's more than enough sheep in this life," she told her husband. "Just let the boy be." George later said, "My mum did encourage me. Perhaps most of all by never discouraging me from anything I wanted to do. . . . If you tell kids not to, they're going to do it in the end anyway. . . . They let me stay out all night

and have a drink when I wanted to." There were limits, however, to what his parents would allow. Though Harrison was a successful art student, he failed most of his other courses, prompting one schoolmaster to remark that he "made no contribution to school life." Harrison's high school, the Liverpool Institute, held him back a year, though he declined to tell his parents. He would spend afternoons visiting friends or movie theaters. When his parents finally discovered his deceit, they weren't so much angry as practical: Since Harrison was no longer in school and not anxious to return, it was time for him to find a job. At his father's insistence, Harrison accepted an apprenticeship as an electrician at a Liverpool department store, Blackler's.

Harrison found the job tedious. He didn't want to be an electrician. He didn't want to be a laborer. By this time, a British pop star named Lonnie Donegan was helping forge a homegrown response to American rockabilly with a trend called skiffle–a merger of American folk and black forms with country textures and a distinctly British cadence.

Harrison, Sutcliffe and Lennon, at a fairgrounds in Hamburg, Germany, 1960. It was their first formal shoot; photographer Astrid Kirchherr later became romantically involved with Sutcliffe.

The vogue eventually became so popular that several young Liverpool males began sporting guitars about town, simply as fashion wear. When Harrison's mother noticed he was constantly drawing sketches of guitars, she bought an inexpensive acoustic for him. He often stayed up through the night, trying to master chords, country-western fingerpicking patterns and rock & roll riffs, and before long, he bought a more professional Hofner model. While riding on his father's bus, Harrison had already met another Liverpool rock & roll fan, Paul McCartney, who was a little older than Harrison. McCartney started studying guitar with Harrison at the Harrisons' home. He was stunned at Harrison's facility on the instrument–he could play fleet rockabilly and country riffs, and McCartney taught him some of the more complex jazz chords and riffs of gypsy guitarist Django Reinhardt. Harrison, in turn, was impressed by McCartney's range and force as a vocalist–his ability to mimic the throat-busting yowls of Little Richard, as well as his talent for memorizing and conveying pop standards and ballads. The two became close friends, hitchhiking on weekends with their guitars, practicing constantly, sometimes sleeping on sand or sidewalks after a long night of trying to copy the style of Carl Perkins or emulate the powerful yet dreamy vocal styles of the Everly Brothers and Buddy Holly. After seeing Holly and the Crickets at Liverpool's Empire Theatre, McCartney thought he and Harrison should form a band of their own. Harrison, though, was content with his role as a sideman and occasional singer.

For the next year or two, Harrison played in pickup bands–a short-lived skiffle outfit, the Rebels, and the Les Stewart Quartet. Meantime, McCartney had become enamored of another local skiffle-based group, the Quarry Men, led by a brash yet charismatic rhythm guitarist and singer, John Lennon. Lennon had an arrogant exterior–he was sarcastic, even rude, but it was hard to say whether these traits were signs of his confidence or vulnerability. He was also a respected student at Liverpool's Art College, though he had little patience for art school pretensions. He was another one of the local roughs who dressed as a teddy boy, and it seemed to many that to get close to him you had accept that he carried a chip on his shoulder and could be sardonic or mean without notice. Though he'd grown up in relative middle-class luxury, he wanted to be seen as a common type with a street temperament. McCartney was more conventional and prudent in his manners, but Lennon's talent and showmanship fascinated McCartney, and soon Lennon accepted him as a member of the Quarry Men, where McCartney effectively became second-in-command. As time went along, McCartney began to lobby Lennon to bring Harrison into the Quarry Men, as well. Lennon was as impressed as McCartney by Harrison's faculty on guitar, but he was leery of accepting Harrison as a peer. Harrison was three years younger than Lennon, and Lennon told McCartney he wasn't sure he wanted to let a "baby" into the group. Also, Lennon was annoyed that Harrison would tag along like an uninvited kid brother in social situations–such as when Lennon was seeing his girlfriend, Cynthia Powell. But Lennon's estimation of Harrison began to turn around when Harrison showed up at the house where Lennon lived with his aunt Mimi and she refused to let the scruffy-looking Harrison enter her tidy home. "And why not, Mimi?" Lennon asked. "Too common for the likes of such a grand lady as you?" Lennon appreciated that Harrison's mother welcomed the young musicians into her house to practice without condescension, and after Lennon's mother, Julia, was killed in a car accident, he was grateful when Harrison visited to console him. Lennon finally caved in: Harrison was allowed to join the group. The only catch was, the Quarry Men were breaking up just as Harrison enlisted.

By the late 1950s and early 1960s, Liverpool had a brimming pop scene, made up of bands playing tough and exuberant blues and R&B-informed rock & roll, a boisterous movement that soon became known as the Merseyside scene. Numerous clubs opened up in the area, featuring such acts as Billy Fury, Gerry Marsden and the Pacemakers, and Rory Storm and the Hurricanes (who featured the flash drummer Richard Starkey, working under the stage name of Ringo Starr). Though the Quarry Men were defunct, the new core team of John Lennon, Paul McCartney and George Harrison remained committed as a determined music unit. Other members came and went, while the group searched for a new name. One possibility: Johnny and the Moondogs. Another: the Silver Beatles (Lennon favored the peculiar spelling of the last name in part because Merseyside bands were becoming known as Beat groups, and also because he, Harrison and McCartney were fans of Jack Kerouac's *On the Road* and the Beat movement).

Finally, a shorter name evolved: the Beatles. An art school friend of Lennon's, Stu Sutcliffe, joined the new group as bassist. Neither Harrison nor McCartney was thrilled with Sutcliffe's addition: Sutcliffe drew too much of Lennon's attention for the liking of either one, and they also considered him a limited musician. Instead, they lobbied for McCartney as bassist—but at the start (and for many years to come), the Beatles were in effect led by John Lennon. Sutcliffe notwithstanding, the main musical dynamic in the group was developing between Lennon and McCartney: They sang most of the leads on the group's ever-growing body of rock & roll covers, and they were starting to compose songs of their own. In fact, they had formed a handshake deal: The two would share songwriting credits as a team of Lennon-McCartney for any songs they wrote jointly or apart. This left Harrison as an odd man out: He had been closer to McCartney for longer, and he was captivated by Lennon's charisma, but he knew he was losing McCartney's loyalty to Lennon. Also, Harrison had no burning desire to be a songwriter. Lennon would allow him the occasional lead vocal and in-strumental, but Harrison quickly became subordinate in the Beatles. By the time his position changed in that regard, much about the group and the world they occupied would change as a result.

Still, Harrison's tenure as a Beatle seemed safe, if only because neither Lennon nor McCartney (or for that matter any other Merseyside musician) could match his finesse as an ensemble guitarist—his keen instinct for the right textures and fills that gave the Beatles' early performances such drive. As a result, a certain dynamic developed among the three initial key members: Lennon and McCartney were the band's center of attention and impetus; Harrison saw himself as along for the fun and exploration. The group viewed its first notable tour—playing Scotland in May 1960—as a likely big break, but when they arrived home and found that their best gig was backing a stripper, Harrison was disheartened. "It was work," he later said, "but definitely not what any of us had in mind when we got together. As for me, I was just about convinced it was never going to happen, which gave me great reason for concern. After all, the only other reasonable alternative was to just go out and find a real job. Frankly, that was something all of us dreaded."

Later in 1960, the Beatles' forecast improved when they found a steady drummer: Pete Best. The Beatles discovered that Liverpool's female fans thought Best was the group's sexiest member, plus Best's mother, Mona, owned a local club that the band could play at any time. Best, however, was a bit aloof—he didn't share in the group's easy camaraderie—and, like Sutcliffe, he was regarded as a limited musician.

In the late summer, a Liverpool entrepreneur, Allan Williams, booked the Beatles into a season-long stint of club shows in Hamburg, Germany. Hamburg was an excitable and diverse scene—full of thugs, prostitutes and drug dealers on one hand and home to a budding intellectual movement on the other. The Beatles managed to find acceptance among both factions: The tougher sorts supplied them with sex and drugs (the Beatles were playing eight-hour sets daily at such clubs as the Indra and the Kaiserkeller, and they became fond of mixing Preludin—a form of speed—with German beer to fuel their increasingly hectic live shows). In addition, the art and existentialist crowd found something daring about the band and adopted the Beatles as a sensation. In particular, artist Klaus Voormann (who later designed some of the Beatles' graphics and eventually played bass on various members' solo projects) and photographer Astrid Kirchherr took the group under their wing. Harrison formed a crush on Kirchherr, and although she thought Harrison was maybe the sweetest-tempered member of the group, she entered into an affair with Sutcliffe. Kirchherr also was the person who introduced the Beatles to their new shag hairstyle–first adopted by Sutcliffe and Harrison.

Harrison once called the Beatles' Hamburg tenure the only "higher education" of his younger life. In addition to the drugs and sex (both of which were plentiful and reportedly diverse), the Beatles would soon grow accustomed to playing for enthusiastic–even brutal–audiences. There were fistfights in the crowd nearly every night, and all the members related how they had witnessed bludgeonings and stabbings as they wisely kept the beat steady, grinding out their sets. On one occasion, McCartney was assaulted with a table. Another time, they watched as one hapless audience member was skewered in the neck with a meat hook and thrown into the street. Lennon wasn't always crazy about the German audiences he played to and sometimes mocked them as "Nazi bastards," to Harrison's delight.

While in Germany, they learned to play a vast repertoire of rock & roll but also grasped how to pace their sets with such novelty songs as "Sheik of Araby," and standards like "September Song" and "Summertime." Two other important things happened to the Beatles during this initial Hamburg visit: For one, they understood that becoming a tighter band was the key to becoming more popular, and that meant recognizing that neither drummer Pete Best nor bassist Stu Sutcliffe would likely survive Lennon, McCartney and Harrison's ambitions. Most important, the Beatles got thrown out of the country–ostensibly because of Harrison. When the group accepted a position at Hamburg's hottest venue, the Top Ten, the Kaiserkeller's owner claimed they owed him an exclusive arrangement and retaliated by notifying local authorities that George Harrison was under the age of eighteen and thereby was playing adult clubs illegally. Within twenty-four hours, the police raided the Beatles' hotel, "looking for the one called Harrison." Lennon replied, "What the fuck do you want him for? He hasn't

done anything." Harrison was deported, and only Astrid Kirchherr and Stu Sutcliffe accompanied him to the train station. "He looked so lost and pathetic standing there on the platform holding his battered guitar case," said Kirchherr. "Tears were welling up in his eyes."

Harrison arrived back in Liverpool in December 1960. The city looked bleak at that time of year, and Harrison later said he felt bleak. He wasn't confident that Lennon and McCartney would keep a place for him in the group. He walked the streets of his hometown, feeling like a washout–a defeated Beatle. Despite everything that would happen in the years ahead, in some ways Harrison never shook the depression that accompanied him back to Liverpool that Christmas season.

* ⊨ * ⊳ *

SOON ENOUGH, McCartney, Lennon, Sutcliffe and Best joined Harrison back in Liverpool, also as deportees. McCartney and Best, according to the German police, had set fire to the place where they bunked while playing the Kaiserkeller–perhaps as vengeance for Harrison being thrown out of the country. Sutcliffe soon quit the band, returning to Hamburg and Kirchherr, which allowed McCartney to become the bassist. The Beatles were now a quartet. And as Harrison and the others looked about at the even more burgeoning Liverpool beat scene, they realized their prospects might be better than ever. They were no longer just a band of skiffle hopefuls. As a result of their intense Hamburg performances they had transformed into the Mersey scene's most soulful rock & roll band.

Once more the Beatles began playing Liverpool's clubs, but to notably different effect: The crowds–particularly the young females–were now ecstatic in their devotion to the group. The Beatles may have left Hamburg as failures but they now ruled their home scene, and they placed first in local polls as the best Merseyside band. The group booked itself into the Cavern, a jazz club in a dank and airless cellar, where it packed the place for both lunch hour and evening shows (eventually, the Beatles played more than two hundred shows at the Cavern). Liverpool's enthusiasm for them was unbounded–and unmatched in the region's entertainment history. While on a brief return trip to Germany (after Harrison had turned eighteen, and the arson charge against McCartney and Best was forgotten), the Beatles recorded some sessions with Tony

Sheridan—a British pop star who had relocated to Hamburg—and cut a few tracks of their own.

According to legend, one Saturday morning in 1961, a young customer entered a record store called NEMS, "The Finest Record Selection in the North," on Whitechapel, a busy road in the heart of Liverpool's stately commercial district. The young man asked store manager Brian Epstein for a new single, "My Bonnie," by the Beatles (its flip side was a Harrison-Lennon instrumental, "Cry for a Shadow"). Epstein replied that he had never heard of the record—indeed, had never heard of the band, which he took to be an obscure, foreign pop group. The customer,

Opposite: July 1966: "I used to try and get George to rebel with me," said Lennon. "I'd say, 'We don't need these fucking little suits. Let's chuck them out the window.'" Following: Beatlemania.

Raymond Jones, pointed out the front window, across Whitechapel, where Stanley Street ran into a murky-looking alley area. Around that corner, he told Epstein, down a small lane known as Mathew Street, the Beatles—perhaps the most popular of Liverpudlian rock & roll groups—were performing afternoons at the Cavern. A few days later, prompted by more requests, Epstein made that journey around Stanley onto Mathew and down the clammy steps into the Cavern. At first, Epstein—a neat man given to sharp suits and ties—was appalled by the rowdy appearance of the band, and he couldn't fathom the reaction of the young audience around him, their almost hysterical commotion. Then, something in Epstein clicked. He saw a vision for his future and for theirs. And as we now know, he saw a vision for the future of us all.

When Epstein made his way backstage to meet the band, Harrison greeted him curtly: "What brings Mr. Epstein here?" They found out soon enough. A month later at Pete Best's house they entered into a management agreement with Brian Epstein. With Epstein's small trek to the Cavern, modern pop culture turned its most eventful corner.

From that point on, a lot happened—and happened remarkably fast. Some of it wasn't pretty: Epstein eventually fired Pete Best, to the outrage of the group's Liverpool fans (in fact, the news was met with a genuine street riot). Best's replacement was Rory Storm's old drummer, Ringo Starr, who would soon tell the *New Musical Express* that he was "lucky to be on their wavelength. . . . I

had to join them as people as well as a drummer." Some of what happened was tragic: Stu Sutcliffe died of a brain hemorrhage in Hamburg, leaving the group shaken. And some of what happened was simply the stuff of extraordinary fortune and legend: In July 1962, after being turned down by many London labels, Epstein secured a recording contract with EMI's Parlophone producer George Martin. By October, the four-piece ensemble had broken into Britain's Top Twenty with a folkish rock song, "Love Me Do." The song began a momentum that would forever shatter the American grip on the U.K. pop charts.

A year after the release of "Love Me Do," the Beatles had six singles active in Britain's Top Twenty all in the same week, including the top three positions—an unprecedented and still unduplicated feat. In the process, Lennon and McCartney had grown enormously as writers—in fact, they were already one of the best composing teams in pop history—and the group itself had upended the local pop scene, establishing a hierarchy of longhaired male ensembles, playing a pop-wise but hardbashing update of 1950s-style rock & roll. But there was more to it than pop success: The Beatles were simply the biggest explosion England had witnessed in modern history, short of war. In less than a year, they had transformed British pop culture and had redefined not only its intensities and possibilities but turned it into a matter of nationalistic impetus.

Then, on February 9, 1964, TV variety-show kingpin Ed Sullivan presented the Beatles for the first time to a mass American audience, and it proved to be an epochal moment. On the flight over to the U.S., the group was nervous—George Harrison in particular. "America's got everything," he said to the others. "Why should they want us?" When the group's plane landed at New York City's JFK Airport, there was such a large turnout of spectators that the band assumed that President Lyndon Johnson must have been coincidentally arriving at the airport at the same time. After a crazed and hilarious press conference (one reporter asked, "Why don't you smile, George?" Harrison replied, "I'll hurt my lips"), the band's press officer rushed them to their hotel. Epstein and the others were concerned: Harrison had the flu, and it was possible he might not be able to make their TV appearance or first few U.S. dates. His sister, Louise, who now lived in the U.S., moved into his hotel suite and, with

the help of a lot of tea and medications, nursed him enough so that the group could make its American debut.

The *Sullivan* appearance drew more than seventy million viewers—the largest TV audience ever, at that time—an event that cut across divisions of style and region and drew new divisions of era and age, an event that, like Presley, made rock & roll seem an irrefutable opportunity. Within days it was apparent that not just pop style but a whole dimension of youth society had been recast—that a genuine upheaval was under way, offering a frenetic distraction to the dread that had set into America after the assassination of President John F. Kennedy and a renewal of the wounded ideal that youthfulness carried our national hope. Elvis Presley had shown us how rebellion could be fashioned into eye-opening style; the Beatles were showing us how style could take on the impact of cultural revelation—or at least how a pop vision might be forged into an unimpeachable consensus. Virtually overnight, the Beatles' arrival in the American consciousness announced that not only the music and times were changing, but that we were changing, as well. Everything about the band—its look, sound, style and abandon—made plain that we were entering a different age, that young people were free to redefine themselves in completely new terms.

Before they were Beatles: With fellow Quarry Men Lennon and McCartney, in the late Fifties. "At that age," Harrison said, "anybody who is into music you buddy with instantly."

✳ ⤙ ✳ ⤚ ✳

THAT'S ONE VERSION of the Beatles' early story—the miracle, rags-to-riches version. It's hardly inaccurate, but it's hardly the full story. Perhaps it isn't fair to call it the Beatles' story—perhaps it's more exact to call it the public story, our version of the fairy tale. There was also the internal experience of that adventure, and some forty years later it remains surprising that there are key details—a psychic and emotional landscape—that only an ever-dwindling number of people truly know well. As the Beatles themselves grew fond of saying, nobody knew their experience in the way they did and therefore all biographies and essays have been speculative at best. And yet none of the four men who lived within that matchless twentieth-century exploit ever wrote a full-scale, revealing autobiography. Years later, when McCartney, Harrison and Starr cowrote their narrative (with posthumous

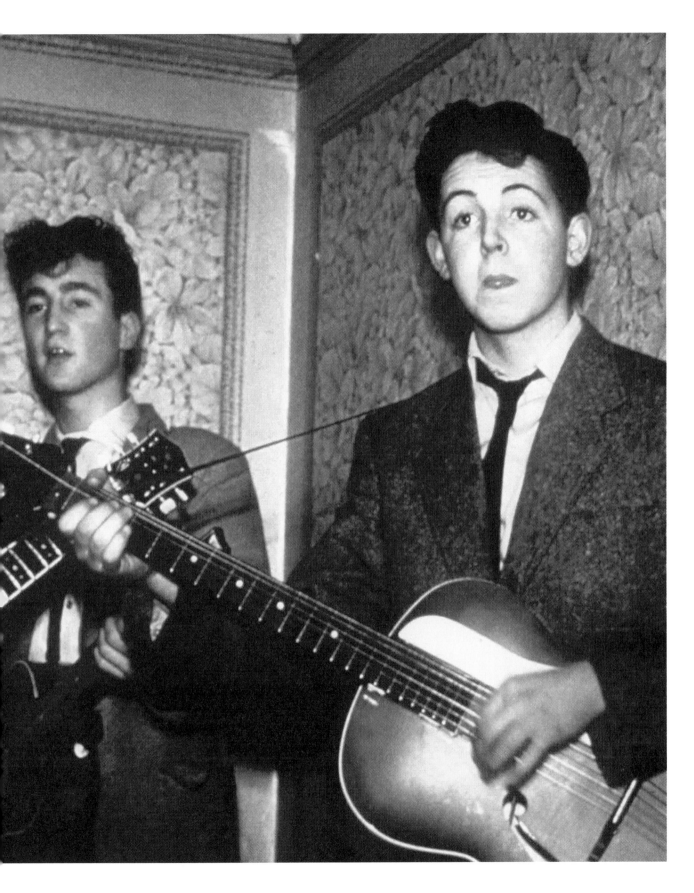

contributions by John Lennon), *The Beatles Anthology,* the storytellers clearly cut some of history's rougher corners a bit clean. Perhaps the single most striking hard truth to emerge from *Anthology* was that there was a great deal of pain involved in being the Beatles, and that pain started much earlier than many of us might have realized. The most notoriously publicized aspect of the Beatles' anguish was, of course, the bitter rift between Lennon and McCartney at the Beatles' end–but it is likely that while the group was intact, nobody within it may have suffered greater grievances than George Harrison.

What accounted for that hurt? In part, it stemmed from the subsidiary role in which Harrison found himself in relation to Lennon and McCartney. Though Harrison contributed significantly to some of the most important and memorable aspects of the Beatles' music–for example, the backward-guitar effects on "I'm Only Sleeping" and the innovative use of controlled feedback on "Yes It

Harrison and Pattie Boyd on the set of 'A Hard Day's Night,' where they first met in March 1964. The couple was married on January 21, 1966. McCartney was the only Beatle to attend.

Is," to say nothing of the sitar phrases that imbued "Norwegian Wood" with both a haunting and witty quality– Harrison remained perpetually in McCartney and Lennon's shadow, not only in

that pair's view, but in producer George Martin's, as well. Martin sometimes criticized Harrison's tuning and timing in the studio–even in the presence of a reporter. Much of the problem owed to Harrison's slow growth as a songwriter. Lennon and McCartney not only wrote the group's essential catalogue, but were–along with George and Ira Gershwin, Duke Ellington and Billy Strayhorn, and Richard Rodgers and his partners Lorenz Hart and Oscar Hammerstein–among the greatest and most prolific pop songwriting teams of the century. Up until *Revolver*–the Beatles' seventh album–Harrison had composed only a handful of songs and sang lead on relatively few (Lennon, for one, didn't think much of Harrison's voice). Harrison later said that he was reluctant to present his songs to the band. "The hang-up of my playing my songs to John and Paul always used to hold me back," he told *New Musical Express* in 1969, "because I knew how it would sound finished and I had to try to convince them in one play. For that reason, there are a lot of numbers of mine that I decided not to do anything about. It was a shyness, a withdrawal,

and I always used to take the easy way out." Another time, Harrison justified his reluctance by saying, "My part in the Beatles was I never wanted to be the one in the front." Yet even Lennon admitted that Harrison would never have been granted that chance for more than a song or two. Lennon told ROLLING STONE that Harrison was "like a bloody kid, hanging around all the time. It took me years to start considering him as an equal."

Another factor that made Beatlemania so troubling for George Harrison was in fact the mania. More than any other Beatle, he came to despise the quality and fervor of attention that the band received. By the end of their first American tour, according to Geoffrey Giuliano's *Dark Horse: The Life and Art of George Harrison,* Harrison was disillusioned with the inanity of fame. On the flight back to England, after the Beatles conquered America, Giuliano writes that Harrison told his band mates, "How fuckin' stupid it all is. All that big hassle to make it, only to end up as performing fleas." This feeling never left Harrison. In *Anthology,* Harrison related how, during a tense appearance in Japan, every time an unexpected loud sound occurred, the band members would look around to see which of them had been shot. Harrison also disclosed his anger about the Beatles not being able to control their own schedules or movements during their hectic tours, and also told how, in 1964, he insisted that the Beatles not participate in a ticker-tape parade planned for a San Francisco appearance. "It was only . . . a year," he said, "since they had assassinated Kennedy. . . . I could just imagine how mad it is in America." Years later, he told ROLLING STONE, "I was getting very nervous. . . . I didn't like the idea of being too popular." Later, when Harrison started to date model Pattie Boyd, he had to deal with the resentments of female fans who physically attacked Boyd, calling her demeaning names. There was no question that the Beatles were at the eye of a tremendous storm of public feeling, and though in *Anthology* Harrison claimed they were the sanest people in that scenario, it's also clear that their fame had isolated them from some of the meaning and pleasure of their experience. In Harrison's mind, the group's audience became an enclosing and demanding reality, always wanting, often threatening, rarely understanding enough. "They used us as an excuse to go mad, the world did," he said, "and then they blamed it on us."

By the time of the band's 1965 tours in the U.S. and

elsewhere, Harrison was starting to make a case for the band to stop traveling and playing live so much. He believed it was only a matter of time before something irreparable would happen. The 1966 world tour only underscored Harrison's claims. When the Beatles failed to show up for a command audience in the Philippines with President Ferdinand Marcos, the band felt lucky to leave the country without serious harm. "They were waiting for us to retaliate," Harrison said of the guards who bullied them at the Manila airport, "so that they could finish us off. I was terrified." Later, at a press conference, Harrison told reporters, "We're going to have a couple of weeks to recuperate before we go and get beaten up by the Americans." A few days later, John Lennon made his infamous remark to a British reporter that the Beatles were "more popular than Jesus Christ," and the reaction in America was so intense–accompanied by numerous death threats–that Brian Epstein offered to refund all the ticket sales if the U.S. tour could be canceled. It hardly helped secure their safety when Lennon and Harrison spoke up against American involvement in Vietnam, but by then everybody involved in the Beatles agreed that the phenomenon of their public performances was coming to a necessary fast end. The band played its last announced concert on August 29, 1966, at San Francisco's Candlestick Park. On the flight back home to England, Harrison settled into his seat and announced, "Well, that's it. I'm not a Beatle anymore." Not even the three men who knew him best could tell if he was happy or sad in the moments that he uttered that remark.

✳ ⛻ ✳ ⛾ ✳

B UT HARRISON, of course, was still a Beatle. In fact, for the next year or two, being a Beatle would not only become a more fulfilling experience for Harrison, but the Beatles' growth–and how they affected their audience in the late 1960s–would owe as much to his influence as to McCartney and Lennon's.

The first manifestation of this influence–albeit an inadvertent one–was Harrison's role in introducing the Beatles to the hallucinogenic drug LSD. One night in 1966, Harrison and Pattie Boyd and John and Cynthia Lennon accepted the invitation of Harrison's dentist to join him and his wife for a small dinner party. After serving the Beatles drinks, the dentist informed them he had just slipped them some LSD. Harrison and Boyd and the Lennons

grew angry and frightened and left. They ended up visiting nightclubs and driving around London for hours before settling into a safe enclosure. The acid had scared them, but it also beguiled Harrison and Lennon, and they began to take it more regularly. For both men, it was the start of an intense exploration that had philosophical and spiritual aspects to it, and that would provoke immense influence and controversy in the pop world and youth culture. "Up until LSD," Harrison told ROLLING STONE, "I never realized that there was anything beyond this state of consciousness. . . . The first time I took it, it just blew everything away. I had such an overwhelming feeling of well-being, that there was a God, and I could see him in every blade of grass. It was like gaining hundreds of years' experience in twelve hours." Harrison soon married Pattie Boyd–a development he believed was now possible due to how psychedelics had helped him develop.

Traveling with Maharishi Mahesh Yogi, 1967. The next year, the Beatles visited the maharishi's ashram in India. "I knew I needed a mantra," Harrison said.

Harrison's experience with LSD would dovetail influentially with two other quests he had undertaken and would help transform the Beatles' meaning and history. The first was musical: At the suggestion of the Byrds' David Crosby, Harrison sought out the recordings of Indian sitar master Ravi Shankar–a classical virtuoso who occasionally mixed elements of Western music (classical, blues and jazz) into the more ancient form of raga structures. Harrison was fascinated by what he heard, and in time met Shankar and asked to study the instrument with him. Shankar cautioned Harrison that the sitar was an extremely difficult and demanding instrument to master, and that to immerse himself in it properly he should spend time in India. Harrison agreed and paid a visit to Shankar in India–resulting in changes not just for the Beatles but for all of modern pop music. Writing about Harrison's death in the *New York Times*, composer Philip Glass said, "George was among the first Western musicians to recognize the importance of music traditions millenniums old, which themselves had roots in indigenous music, both popular and classical. Using his considerable influence and popularity, he was one of those few who pushed open the door that, until then, had separated the music of much of the world from

the West. . . . He played a major role in bringing several generations of young musicians out of the parched and dying desert of Eurocentric music into a new world."

The beginning of this lifelong friendship with Shankar also provided the foundation for a change in Harrison's worldview. Through Shankar and Indian music, Harrison said, he discovered a new openness to spirituality–especially to ancient Hindu teachings. He began to study the mystical literature of legendary Yogi Paramahansa Yogananda and would also later form a lifelong relationship with Swami Prabhupada and the Krishna Consciousness movement. In the hotbed of late 1960s hippie culture, Harrison's spiritual interest spread like wildfire–to other musicians and groups (including the Beach Boys, Mick Jagger and Donovan) and to much

Lennon and Harrison at Abbey Road in 1967, the year the Beatles recorded 'Sgt. Pepper's.' The album cost twenty-five thousand pounds to make–twenty times the cost of their first album in 1963.

of American and British youth, as well. For most people, of course, sampling ancient scripture like the Bhagavad Gita or the Upanishads, or chanting "Hare Krishna," was simply a vogue of the season. For Harrison (and, in different ways, for Lennon, too) this turn toward the spiritual became permanently transforming.

The combination of all these discoveries–the possibility of finding a connection to a god in oneself and in the world and the rich, complex pleasures of Indian sounds– also bore musical fruit for Harrison. He featured Indian instrumentation on *Revolver*'s "Love You To," on *Sgt. Pepper's Lonely Hearts Club Band*'s longest track, the psalmlike "Within You Without You" ("Forget the Indian music and listen to the melody," Paul McCartney once said about this remarkable recording), and on "The Inner Light" (a devotional on the B side of "Lady Madonna"). For some listeners, these experiments were unbearably pompous and exotic, and yet today they all hold up as not merely adventurous but as enduring musical pleasures. Also, Harrison's openness to new sounds and textures cleared new paths for his rock & roll compositions. His use of dissonance on such tracks as *Revolver*'s "Taxman" and "I Want to Tell You" was revolutionary in popular music—and perhaps more originally creative than the avant-garde mannerisms that Lennon and McCartney borrowed from the music of Karlheinz Stockhausen, Luciano Berio, Edgar Varese and Igor Stravinsky in this same period.

In any event, 1967's *Sgt. Pepper* was an era-defining and form-busting work. To many, it certified that rock was now art and that art was, more than ever, a mass medium. In addition, rock was now filled with not only ideals of defiance, but also with dreams of love, community and spirituality—and it was the possibility of the music as the medium for kinship and growth that would dominate (and later haunt) popular culture through the remainder of the decade. Even the Rolling Stones—who always sang about much darker concerns—would start recording songs about love and altruism. "For a brief while," wrote critic Langdon Winner of the *Sgt. Pepper* era, "the irreparably fragmented consciousness of the West was unified, at least in the minds of the young."

But that blithe center couldn't hold forever. With psychedelia and hippie counterculture at their peak in both England and America in the summer of 1967, Harrison was the only Beatle who decided to visit the scene's ostensible center, the Haight-Ashbury district in San Francisco. According to Geoffrey Giuliano's account, Harrison, Boyd and the Beatles press agent took LSD before wandering into the Haight—and though Harrison remained polite to the young people who surrounded him, he was aghast at what he found. "They are hypocrites," he told *Creem* of his experience with the Haight residents. "I don't mind anybody dropping out of anything, but it's the imposition on somebody else I don't like. I've just realized that it doesn't matter what you are, as long as you work. In fact, if you drop out, you put yourself further away from the goal of life than if you were to keep working."

Harrison later revealed that his acid trip that afternoon was the last one he would take for years to come. He felt he had seen firsthand the wonders of the drug's experience, but also the havoc it might cause for an unready or a naive community. Harrison now realized, he said, how vast the Beatles' influence was on youth, and that he wanted that influence to be more positive. His wife, Pattie, introduced him to the teachings of Maharishi Mahesh Yogi, who had formulated some philosophical (and economic) twists on Hindu teachings. Harrison liked the maharishi's teachings about overcoming human weaknesses through meditation to achieve bliss, and he persuaded the other Beatles to accompany him to one of the teacher's lectures. The Beatles were impressed by what they heard and accepted the maharishi's invitation to attend a sabbatical in Bangor, Wales. Later, the Beatles joined the maharishi for an even more extended study retreat in Rishikesh, but their relationship with the teacher soured when they heard rumors that he had attempted unwelcome sexual advances on a female devotee. Lennon and Harrison confronted the maharishi, pronounced their disdain and then left, despite his pleadings that they reconsider their judgment on him (later in his life Harrison reconciled with the maharishi, though Lennon never did).

But an event more significant to the Beatles' future than their spiritual explorations took place during that first retreat in Bangor. Manager Brian Epstein, who had been scheduled to join them, never showed. Epstein had been a depressed and lonely man for some time, and according to some who knew him, he was afraid that his place in the Beatles' life might be slipping. He had been taking more pills and drinking more, and had attempted to find cures for his depression, to no avail. On August 27, 1967, while the Beatles were with the maharishi in Bangor, they received news that Epstein had been found dead of an overdose of sleeping pills and antidepressants—an accidental suicide, some believed. The Beatles were shell-shocked by the news. Speaking at a hastily assembled press conference in Bangor, Harrison said, "The maharishi told us not to be too overshadowed by grief. . . . I feel my course on meditation here has helped me overcome my grief more easily than before." But the expressions on his and the other Beatles' faces didn't convey any sense of overcoming. As Harrison later admitted, "We didn't know what to do. We were lost."

※ ⋘ ※ ⋙ ※

I T ' S   T R U E that the Beatles were lost without Brian Epstein. At first they tried to manage themselves. They financed and produced their own TV film special, *Magical Mystery Tour.* It made for good music but a disastrous film, and it was the first time the Beatles were ridiculed by critics (the show was considered so bad that it never aired in the United States). They also set up their own recording label and multimedia corporation, Apple, and signed numerous new artists. But between overseeing business affairs and other artists' record productions, trying to create their own music and to fund various experimental philanthropic enterprises (and not-so-philanthropic ambitions, such as a short-lived ambition to own, populate and reign over their own island off Greece), they had stretched themselves too thin, and they almost went bankrupt. Clearly, they needed new management, and Lennon suggested the entertainment industrialist who had seemingly helped the Rolling Stones recover: Allen Klein. Again, this is a period in which much happened with stunning speed and effectiveness in the Beatles' history—but this time little of it was fairy tale; rather, it was a nightmare—and the public and press' backlash against them was often unforgiving. In May 1968, John Lennon began an affair with Yoko Ono—a respected avant-garde artist who had been part of New York's Fluxus movement. Soon after, he left and divorced his wife, Cynthia, and his resulting inseparable closeness with Ono was seen as causing much tension within the Beatles' world.

Also, as the group's members—including Harrison and Starr—began to grow musically, they also began to have little room for one another in their lives and music. The most brilliant yet foreboding example of how the group was splintering came as they were recording a double album, initially titled *A Doll's House,* later called *The Beatles* but better known as the White Album. By this point, the band's members were largely recording as separate individuals or as each other's sidemen. Harrison had written his best body of songs yet—including the lovely "Long Long Long," "All Things Must Pass," "Wah-Wah," "Isn't It a Pity," "Not Guilty," "Something" and "While My Guitar Gently Weeps," but once again he found himself facing the harsh judgments of Lennon, McCartney and producer George Martin. Martin at first thought "Something" sounded too weak and derivative. The one song Harrison expected to receive the most enthusiastic response, "While My Guitar Gently Weeps," left McCartney and Lennon cold when he played a demo for them (the same version that is now regarded as the best track on *Anthology 3*). Harrison was determined to get the song on the new album and laid plans to make it happen: He invited his good friend Eric Clapton to attend and play lead on the session. Clapton panicked at the request. "I can't come," he said. "Nobody's ever played on a Beatles record," but he gave in to Harrison's insistence. Clapton later said he could tell that things were bad within the group—Lennon never appeared for the session—but Harrison's strategy worked: The other Beatles didn't feel they could refuse a track with such a standout guitar solo. "Not Guilty," though, never made the cut—perhaps because it was apparent to everybody that Harrison had aimed the song at Lennon and McCartney.

The Beatles could no longer figure out how to survive each other. McCartney tried to keep the band on course. He wanted to return to touring, but Harrison and Lennon wouldn't consider it. Instead, they agreed to rehearse for a one-time live show at some undisclosed location and to film their rehearsals. A few days into these sessions—which resulted in the album and film *Let It Be*—Harrison had reached a breaking point with McCartney. Lennon had now more or less abdicated his leadership, and Harrison felt McCartney was trying to exert too much control over the band, even dictating guitar parts. After one argument between the two over whether the Beatles should play a live show in Tunisia, Harrison told McCartney—on camera—"You're so full of shit, man," and for a brief time Harrison quit the band. He was back shortly and the band played its impromptu live show on Apple Corp.'s rooftop, but little magic made it to the album of *Let It Be.* There were other trying matters: Lennon and Ono were arrested for drug possession and so were Harrison and Boyd, plus there was the arrival and bullying manner of new manager Allen Klein (now entrusted by Lennon, Harrison and Starr, despised by McCartney, and eventually sued by all). The decisive rift in the Beatles occurred in the relationship between McCartney and Lennon due to arguments about Klein and creative directions.

It was only a matter of time before somebody would bolt the group for good, and yet, despite all the growing bad will, its members agreed to set aside their squabbles and enter the studio for what would be the last time, to record one of their most ingenious and satisfying albums, *Abbey Road.* Harrison had two songs on this final set. "Here Comes the Sun," a song written in Clapton's garden, in reaction to the darkness that was clearly setting in on the Beatles, became Harrison's equivalent to "Let It

Be" or "Imagine": a graceful anthem of hope amid difficult realities. Also, "Something" finally got a fair hearing. George Martin later admitted that maybe he had underestimated Harrison: "I think it's possible he'll emerge as a great musician and composer next year. He's got tremendous drive and imagination, and also the ability to show himself as a great composer on the par with Lennon and McCartney." Lennon, though he agreed that "Something" was *Abbey Road*'s best song, was a bit more roundabout in his 1980 comments to David Sheff for *Playboy:* "He [Harrison] was working with two brilliant songwriters, and he learned a lot from us. I wouldn't have minded being George, the invisible man."

"Something" would be George Harrison's first A side on a Beatles single and would quickly reach the Number One position on America's charts. It would also be Harrison's only prominent Beatles single. In April 1970, Paul McCartney served suit to dissolve the band. The Beatles were no more. The group had been marked by the emerging cynicism of the era. They were already regarding one another as creations of undeserved hype. For everything they had once been—lively, novel and uplifting—the Beatles ended as bitter, mutually unbelieving strangers.

It would be almost a quarter of a century later—and an excess of grief, anger, fear and blood—before they would release new music together under the name of the most famous and beloved band in popular music history.

* ⌖ * ⌖ *

POPULAR HISTORY has told us for years that it was the increasing rivalry between Paul McCartney and John Lennon that ended the Beatles—that McCartney wanted to dominate the group, or that Lennon estranged McCartney and the others with his intense love for Ono, or that they had simply outgrown their mutual artistic interests and their need for one another. Lennon had walked from the group before McCartney had, but McCartney and Allen Klein persuaded him to wait until the band's final product was released before making his announcement. Lennon was furious then when McCartney seemingly pulled a fast one: On the eve of the release of *Let It Be* (recorded prior to *Abbey Road,* but held back for remixing and for a final film edit), he issued a press release for his own first solo work, *McCartney,* in which he announced that the Beatles were finished, and that, no, he didn't think he would

miss Ringo Starr on the drums. Lennon felt McCartney had betrayed them all—though he also wished he'd been the one to use the band's breakup to his own commercial advantage. Harrison felt McCartney had been ungracious, but he was relieved that the band's division was official. "The split-up of the Beatles satisfied me more than anything else in my career," he said, according to biographer Geoffrey Giuliano.

It is possible, though, that if Lennon and McCartney's drama hadn't been so bitter and public, then what Harrison was about to do on his own may have been effectively enough to make the Beatles beside the point. Indeed, it was something far more enterprising than even Lennon or McCartney had envisioned for themselves. Harrison had been seen as a lucky tag-along by George Martin, as a bothersome but esteemed kid brother by Lennon and McCartney, and as "the quiet one" by a press that never seemed to grasp his dry, derisive wit or his real, deepening interest in Eastern philosophy. In truth, all these miscalculations would benefit Harrison in the short run, though they also left deep and lasting wounds.

By the time the Beatles were in their breakup stage, Harrison was clearly aspiring to something extraordinary. He had already recorded two solo efforts for Apple and its subsidiary label, Zapple: *Wonderwall,* a soundtrack to a rarely seen film, though Harrison's music was inventive and the album remains among his best works, and *Electronic Sounds,* haphazard recordings he made with the first Moog synthesizer imported into England—an album he later called "rubbish." Harrison had also recorded an album's worth of duets, originals and covers with Bob Dylan (including a cover of Paul McCartney's "Yesterday" that seemed designed to finish the song for good). The sessions have never been released, though Harrison drew on some of the songs over the years.

More important, Harrison had a considerable backlog of songs that had been left off of earlier Beatles albums, and he was writing more new ones on a regular basis. Harrison decided that it was time to see if these songs could stand on their own—especially outside the context of the Beatles. He recruited a stellar group of musicians, including drummers Ringo Starr, Jim Gordon and Alan White; bassists Klaus Voormann and Carl Radle; keyboardists Gary Wright, Bobby Whitlock, Billy Preston and Gary Brooker; guitarists Eric Clapton and Dave Mason; horn players Jim Price and Bobby Keys; and pedal-steel player Pete Drake. He also persuaded famed, idiosyncratic producer Phil Spector (who had remixed *Let It Be* and was also working with John Lennon on his first post-Beatles album) to help oversee the effort, along with orchestral arranger John Barham. Harrison relished not having to submit his songs to Lennon, McCartney and Martin for approval. He had more than enough strong songs—forty, he claimed—to make a multirecord set, but he was also intent on letting some of the tracks stretch to a greater length with fuller band treatments (including a robust horn section) than would have been possible with the Beatles. Harrison appeared to be enjoying his best musical experience, and he was flattered and bolstered by his new accompanists. "Having played with other musicians," he would tell *Melody Maker* years later, "I don't think the Beatles were that good."

The album, however, would take longer to record than Harrison anticipated. His mother, Louise, had developed a brain tumor, and Harrison was committed to helping her recovery. "The doctor was an idiot and was saying, 'There's nothing wrong with her, she's having some psychological trouble,' " he later told *Musician.* "When I went to see her, she didn't even know who I was. I had to punch the doctor out. . . . She recovered a little bit for about seven months. And during that period, my father, who'd taken care of her, had suddenly exploded with ulcers and was in the same hospital. I was running back and forth to do this record. . . . I wrote the song ['Deep Blue'] . . . at home one exhausted morning. . . . It's filled with frustration and gloom of going to these hospitals and the feeling of disease that permeated the atmosphere. Not being able to do anything for suffering family or loved ones is an awful experience." Louise Harrison died on July 7, 1970, with Harrison at her bedside, reading passages to her from a text about the Bhagavad Gita, commenting on the sacred book's views of death as a changeover rather than a termination.

By late November, Harrison had finished his album, *All Things Must Pass.* It was an unprecedented feat—the first three-LP set in rock & roll (it was reissued in 2001 as a boxed two-CD package—and went to the Number One album position in both the U.S. and England. It would remain on the charts for most of the following year, and it

enjoyed better reviews than McCartney's or Lennon's first solo efforts, which were seen as slight in McCartney's case, and as acerbic and indulgent in Lennon's case. "I remember John was really negative," Harrison told *Crawdaddy.* "John just saw the album cover and said, 'He must be mad, putting three records out. And look at the picture on the front, he looks like an asthmatic Leon Russell.' " It is possible that the cover irritated Lennon because it depicted Harrison seated on a landscape surrounded by four lazy gnomes, who served to represent the fallen Beatles. "There was a lot of negativity going down," Harrison continued. "I just felt that whatever happened, whether it was a flop or success, I was gonna go on my own just to have a bit of peace of mind." *All Things Must Pass* was indeed a success, despite its extravagances. It was musically resourceful and thematically broad—featuring loving yet saddened send-offs to the Beatles ("Wah-Wah" and "Isn't It a Pity"), evocative warnings about the dangers of false values ("Beware of Darkness") and surprisingly beautiful Dylan tribute collaborations ("I'd Have You Anytime" and "If Not for You"). The album also produced Harrison's first solo Number One single, the irresistible devotional "My Sweet Lord"—a song as pervasive on radio

Their final photo shoot: August 1969, at Lennon's new home, Tittenhurst Park. "The Beatles had to self-destruct," Harrison said. "It was stifling us."

and in youth consciousness as anything the Beatles had produced, though also a song that would later contribute to Harrison's calamity and withdrawal.

In all, as Anthony DeCurtis wrote in 2000 in ROLLING STONE, "George Harrison had the most to gain from the breakup of the Beatles"—and he gained it. George Harrison was now the most respected member of his former group. He offered a cautious yet optimistic and tender worldview that stood in stark contrast to the ugly dissolution of the Beatles and the defeated idealism that then characterized so much of rock & roll culture. Harrison told a British newspaper that he now believed "music should be used for the perception of God, not jitterbugging." To be sure, it was a preachy and somewhat misplaced sentiment. Jitterbugging can bring one every bit as close to enlightenment as singing hymns, and Harrison would make more than his share of frivolous music in years to come. But in the darkness at the end of the 1960s and the beginning of the 1970s—after the hippie

dream had turned to cynicism and exploitation, after the horror wrought by the Charles Manson family in Los Angeles and the fatal debacle of the Rolling Stones' free concert at Altamont, as the Vietnam War continued to make a callous sacrifice of thousands and thousands of American and Southeast Asian lives, and as the dark years of Richard Nixon were on the rise–it was refreshing to hear a man who had once been viewed as a side talent rise to his moment and find a voice of liberation. It was a voice willing to face the "hopelessness" he saw around him "in the dead of night" and, for one majestic moment, beat back the fears that had long consumed him. George Harrison was out of the shadows–at least for the moment. No matter what else might be said about him in the years ahead, he made the finest solo work that any ex-Beatle ever produced. And what was more, he was about to top himself.

* ⤙ * ⤚ *

IN MARCH 1970, Harrison and Boyd bought Friar Park–a sprawling, eccentric nineteenth-century mansion and estate on the outskirts of Henley, England. Harrison built a state-of-the-art recording studio in his new home, and he grew to develop a fixation about the property, tending personally to its flower gardens and uncovering hidden underground water grottoes and secret passageways that had been hidden for the better part of a century.

In 1971, John Lennon (who now admitted that *All Things Must Pass* wasn't so bad and that he preferred it to the music his former songwriting partner was recording) invited Harrison to participate in the sessions for his own second, more ambitious solo album, *Imagine.* By this time, the chasm between Lennon and McCartney had reached new depths, and Lennon's vitriol knew few limits. Two of *Imagine'*s most caustic songs–"Crippled Inside" and "How Do You Sleep?"–were aimed at McCartney. Lennon and Harrison had some differences, but they still enjoyed working together, and they still shared a common front against McCartney. Harrison played on both of Lennon's anti-Paul diatribes, many years later telling *Musician:* "I enjoyed 'How Do You Sleep.' I liked being on that side of it, rather than on the receiving end."

Also in 1971, Harrison's old friend and master Ravi Shankar came to him with a request. In March of that year, East Pakistan–now an independent nation called Bangladesh–had been sundered by a cyclone, and a Pak-

istan Muslim military force took advantage of the disaster by mounting an attack on the Hindu population that opposed a Pakistani dictatorship. Between the war and the natural disaster, millions of Hindus were fleeing to India for sanctuary, but India couldn't afford them relief. Members of Shankar's own family had been among the casualties and refugees, and Shankar appealed to Harrison to help him find a way to raise both awareness and funds to help deal with the tragedy. Harrison had been loathe to perform again in any high-profile way, but he thought that the quickest and most effective means to bring money and attention to the problem was to stage a benefit concert and follow it with the release of a recording and film. Still, to achieve the kind of attention that both he and Shankar hoped for, it would have to be quite a concert–something akin to a Beatles reunion. Harrison set aside his misgivings and pursued that possibility but quickly realized it couldn't happen. Reportedly, McCartney delayed on committing himself and Lennon wanted Ono to perform with the band, which Harrison wouldn't allow. Only Ringo Starr was willing to commit his services. Harrison then turned to Allen Klein to book August performance dates at New York City's Madison Square Garden, and Harrison began making calls to musician friends to contribute their time and talent to this event and cause. Harrison's ideal was to present famous and respected talent performing familiar and stirring songs, with top-notch sound. He ended up assembling an orchestra as impressive as the one that had played on *All Things Must Pass.* In addition to Starr, Harrison elicited the support of Eric Clapton, Billy Preston, Leon Russell, Jim Keltner, Klaus Voormann, Badfinger and numerous other musicians and singers, plus producer Phil Spector. But Harrison's fondest hope was to win the involvement of rock & roll's most elusive and esteemed songwriter, Bob Dylan, who had made only three concert appearances since 1966. Dylan was interested, but hesitant. He attended rehearsals, but bristled when Harrison suggested that Dylan sing his earliest anthem, "Blowin' in the Wind." Dylan shot back, "Are you going to sing 'I Want to Hold Your Hand'?" Dylan implied that if he performed at all, he was more inclined to do recent material; like Harrison, he was reluctant to be defined by his past work.

At the first of two concerts on August 1, 1971, Harrison introduced Shankar for an opening set of Indian music. Harrison and his orchestra then took the stage, opening with "Wah-Wah" and "My Sweet Lord." An hour later, after a lovely acoustic rendition of "Here Comes the Sun," Harrison looked to the stage wings. Dylan still hadn't committed himself to performing, and "right up until the moment he stepped onstage, I was not sure he was coming," Harrison said. Dylan strode out from the wings, wearing a denim jacket and harmonica rack, and carrying an acoustic guitar. "I'd like to introduce a friend of us all," Harrison said with obvious glee, and, with Harrison on guitar, Leon Russell on bass and Ringo Starr on tambourine, Dylan performed a stunning and confident set that included "A Hard Rain's A-Gonna Fall" and "Blowin' in the Wind." Harrison accomplished what nobody else had been able to: He convinced Dylan to perform his early folk songs in the city that had given him his greatest triumphs, and three years later when Dylan returned to stages with his own nationwide tour, he attempted to emulate the professionalism that had made the pacing and construction of Harrison's Bangladesh concert such an artistic triumph and historic landmark. There would be other larger benefits in the years to come, including the Live Aid concerts, the Farm Aid series and the recent concerts to benefit the victims of the September 11 attacks. And, it is likely that, sooner or later, another eminent pop-music figure would have taken the step that Harrison did, but it was Harrison who set the model for how to stage a large-scale charitable pop-music entertainment event that could be both a successful fund-raiser and a satisfying concert experience.

Unfortunately, the Concert for Bangladesh immediately ran into problems that impeded Harrison's best intentions. Harrison grew irritated and wary when he felt that various parties were holding up the album's release to figure a way to profit on what would be another three-record set's distribution (Capitol felt that the production costs on the album were enormous). Also, both the American and British tax systems insisted on taking a good deal of the proceeds. It would be more than a decade before Harrison was allowed to present the U.S. Committee for UNICEF with a check that amounted to a much smaller portion of the concert's proceeds than Harrison had hoped for.

Though he found the delay embarrassing and disheartening, Harrison said, "It's nice to know you can achieve these sorts of things, even though the concert was ten years ago, and the public has forgotten about the problems of Bangladesh. The children still desperately need help and the money will have a significant impact." In the late 1980s, when Bob Geldof invited Harrison to take part in the London side of the Live Aid concerts, Harrison wasn't ready to revisit the concert stage, but he offered Geldof something he considered far more valuable: meticulous advice about how to finesse the legal and tax system so that the large funds raised from a charitable entertainment event could be dispersed effectively, without the benefactors having to overcome bureaucratic hindrances.

* ⟝ * ⟞ *

THE FINANCIAL QUAGMIRE that obstructed Harrison's best intentions for the Concert for Bangladesh turned out to be the first major discouragement in Harrison's post-Beatles career, but he was also facing other problems. His marriage to Pattie Boyd was in trouble. Harrison, according to Boyd, had adopted a religious view that sex should only be used for procreation. Boyd felt lonely and distant from her husband, and began a relationship with Eric Clapton that resulted in one of Clapton's most forceful and agonized compositions, "Layla." According to some who saw Harrison during this time, he seemed adrift. It hardly helped matters when, during a dinner with Boyd at Ringo and Maureen Starr's house, Harrison boldly proclaimed that he was in love with Starr's wife. Boyd left the dinner in tears, and Starr didn't know what to say. When Harrison and Maureen reportedly consummated this proposition, the news enraged John Lennon, who reprimanded Harrison, accusing him of virtual incest. Even so, Harrison and Starr kept their friendship. Harrison helped Starr considerably with his most popular solo effort, *Ringo*, writing the hit single "Photograph" for the drummer, and agreeing to contribute guitar parts to the only session that ever featured a reconvened form of the Beatles (though the four members recorded their contributions separately). In fact, Harrison, Lennon and Starr worked jointly in the studio so effectively on *Ringo* that at one point Harrison suggested that the three of them again form a permanent group.

Lennon wouldn't deign to give the suggestion any response–even a refusal. Even so, Harrison would later say, "I'd join a band with John Lennon any day, but I couldn't join a band with Paul McCartney. That's not personal, but from a musical point of view."

Harrison also kept his friendship with Clapton despite Boyd's growing romance with his friend. Later, when the marriage had clearly dissolved and Boyd's affections had shifted to Clapton, the three met to resolve the matter. With Boyd looking on, Harrison said, "Well, I suppose I'd better divorce her." Clapton replied, "Well, that means I've got to marry her." (Boyd and Clapton were wed in 1979, with McCartney, Starr and Harrison–who called himself Clapton's "husband-in-law"–in attendance. The couple later divorced, though Boyd retained a good friendship with both her former husbands.)

In 1973, Harrison released his second studio album, *Living in the Material World.* The collection sold well and produced another Number One single, "Give Me Love (Give Me Peace on Earth)," but critics saw it as a lesser collection than *All Things Must Pass,* and many writers began to react against what they saw as the relentlessly pious nature of Harrison's musical pronouncements. Harrison was prepared for the reaction. He had already told *Melody Maker:* "They feel threatened when you talk about something that isn't *be-bop-a-lula.* And if you say the words *god* . . . or *lord* it makes some people's hair curl." Through it all, though–sex or abstinence, misconstrued pride and equally misunderstood generosity–neither Harrison nor any of the other ex-Beatles could overcome their glorious and now mythic past, nor could they overcome themselves at times. Lennon left Ono for a time and went on a drinking holiday in Los Angeles. Starr and Harrison also found themselves drinking too much, as their marriages struggled. According to friends of the Beatles, the four men often asked others how their former band mates were doing. Both McCartney and Lennon expressed guarded regret that the band had split so determinedly, and McCartney floated the possibility that the two might write together again at some point.

It was in this time and context that George Harrison elected to become the first ex-Beatle to mount a major tour of America, in 1974. The tour was met with strong hopes–despite his personal problems, Harrison still enjoyed considerable public and commercial favor–but that would all change with what became known as the *Dark Horse* tour. Things went badly before the tour even began. Harrison was in the process of launching his own label, Dark Horse Records (distributed by A&M, since Harrison had grown disaffected with EMI after their handling of *The Concert for Bangla Desh*), and he had overextended himself with production and business tasks. He was also hurriedly finishing an album for the tour and assembling a band to begin rehearsals–all in short order. "It is really a test," Harrison told *Melody Maker.* "I either finish the tour ecstatically happy or I'll end up going back into my cave for another five years."

By the first date in Vancouver, B.C., Harrison's voice sounded strained, and it never recovered. Also, some fans and reviewers were put off by the show's mix of pop, Indian music and jazz and took offense at how Harrison had chosen to recast the few Beatles-era songs he performed, including his version of John Lennon's "In My Life" (with the new lyrical twist, "In my life/I've loved God more"). The tour was almost universally savaged by the press, with ROLLING STONE providing some of the most disparaging commentary. "In defense of his tour . . . " one reviewer wrote, "George Harrison has argued that 'If you don't expect anything, life is one big bonus. But when you expect anything, then you can be let down.' So expect nothing–is that the moral of a shriveled career?" Harrison went back and forth during the tour from being philosophical to being defensive. At one press conference he said, "I can see a time when I'd give up this sort of madness." On another occasion he said, "Gandhi says, 'Create and preserve the image of your choice.' The image of my choice is not Beatle George. Why live in the past? Be here now, and now, whether you like me or not, is where I am. Fuck, my life belongs to me. It actually doesn't. It belongs to . . . the Lord Krishna. . . . That's how I feel. I've never been so humble in all my life, and I feel great."

In Washington, D.C., in mid-December, Harrison

"Clapton, Dylan, Ringo," Harrison said of his friends, in 1987, "we're not old. Maybe it's the mellowing process— everybody seems to have gotten so much more at ease."

was invited to the White House to meet with President Gerald Ford. It was a good-tempered visit, and during their conversation Harrison implored the president to consider the case of John Lennon, who had waged a long fight to avoid extradition from the U.S. under the Nixon administration. Two nights later, Lennon visited Harrison backstage at Nassau Coliseum on New York's Long Island, where the two got into an argument, reportedly about the old days, though it was likely an expression of the severe strains Harrison was under at the time. It ended with Harrison yanking Lennon's eyeglasses from his face and throwing them to the floor. Lennon later said that he "saw George going through pain, and I know what pain is, so I let him do it."

Dark Horse, the album, followed the tour and received the worst review that any ex-Beatle had yet endured. Interestingly, today it stands up as one of Harrison's most fascinating works—a record about change and loss, with a radical reworking of the Everly Brothers "Bye Bye Love" that was Harrison's farewell to his marriage. In any case, *Dark Horse* was an embarrassing commercial failure, and between the tour, the dissolution of his marriage and the album's collapse, Harrison withdrew to his home. He claimed that the cumulative disapproval and problems hadn't affected him, but others believe he in fact felt battered. In 1977, looking back on that time of trial, Harrison told *Crawdaddy,* "You either go crackers and commit suicide or you try to realize something and attach yourself to an inner strength."

Harrison found that inner strength in Eastern philosophy. Like the rest of the Beatles, he had great and plentiful opportunities in his life at an early age: He could see any place in the world, own any car or most any property that he fancied, find sex or love on any day, and yet there was something in him that remained lonely and in need, something that even he couldn't always find access to. Hindu precepts gave him a rich opportunity, a way to be in the world but to withdraw from it at the same time; a way to experience pain and yet contemplate it from a different angle. Harrison's religious beliefs helped him survive the Beatles while he was still within their community—and perhaps over time these beliefs helped him survive the Beatles, when, years later, he was constantly reminded that his tenure with the band would always eclipse—or at least set a standard for—every work or performance he might offer. This isn't to say that Harrison's beliefs necessarily made him a "better" man—a man at peace, or a man full of natural beneficence. His convictions didn't make him comfortable with the world or safe from it, and perhaps they didn't always make him comfortable with himself and his own failings. Rather, they seemed to give him a way of continuing despite his conviction that too much of life was hellish and futile.

* ⋉ * ⋊ *

H ARRISON CONTINUED to issue records from time to time and to make occasional public appearances, but the crises he faced in the mid-1970s changed him. Some of those changes were clearly for the better. While forming Dark Horse Records, Harrison met Olivia Arias, who shared some of his interests in spiritual studies. The two became constant companions, and later Olivia helped Harrison treat his depression, which had been exacerbated by heavy drinking and hepatitis. On August 1, 1978, Arias gave birth to Harrison's only child, his son, Dhani, and Olivia and Harrison were married in a secret ceremony the following month, on September 2. "I stopped being as crazy as I used to be," Harrison later said, "because I want this child to have a father a bit longer." (Harrison's own father, Harry, had died earlier that same year, in May.)

Harrison's next two albums—*Extra Texture (Read All About It)* from 1975 and *Thirty-three and 1/3* from 1976— both had rewarding moments (especially *Texture*'s single, "You"), but the context and apparent meanings of popular music were changing. Beatles-related releases now mattered only to the degree that they produced enjoyable sounds, rather than cultural sway. Paul McCartney had enjoyed a run of thriving releases—*Band on the Run, Venus and Mars, At the Speed of Sound*—and pulled off a massively profitable and acclaimed U.S. tour with his post-Beatles band, Wings. But not all of the Beatles' 1970s work enjoyed such consistent reception. For his part, John Lennon had gone into seeming retirement, after he and Yoko Ono reconciled and she gave birth to their son, Sean. Meantime, the pop world had given up not just hope for a fabled Beatles reunion, but also, for a time, in the ongoing significance of their collective or singular works. Rock & roll was still seen as a force that could change individual lives and larger society, but by the late 1970s, the brand of hopefulness that the Beatles had exemplified–and the spiritual transcendence that Harrison's *All Things Must Pass* had apotheosized–was now seen as quaint or ineffectual. The two movements that most changed pop music during this time–punk and disco, both of which Harrison hated–spoke for changing social realities and class conditions that the Beatles seemed unaware of, even though they had grown up in a time and place of similar deprivations and uncertainties.

Also, Harrison faced new and sizeable legal troubles that discouraged his music activity. In 1976, he was sued by Bright Tunes, who owned the copyright for the Chiffons' "He's So Fine." The suit charged that Harrison had lifted the melody and arrangement of "He's So Fine" for "My Sweet Lord." To most sensible observers it seemed like a ludicrous nuisance suit. Pop tunesmiths had been lifting or emulating melodies and arrangements for decades–it was simply an accepted tradition of pop–but the court agreed that Harrison was guilty of "subcon-

scious plagiarism," and ordered him to pay the plaintiff more than a half million dollars. Part of what made this so galling was that by the time the fine was paid, the song was owned by former Beatles manager Allen Klein, who was perhaps seeking a sly revenge after Lennon, Starr and Harrison finally came around to McCartney's view that Klein was not a scrupulous caretaker of the Beatles'

In the early Nineties with son Dhani, who played on "My Sweet Lord (2000)" on the 'All Things Must Pass' reissue

interests. Harrison said the ruling "made me so paranoid about writing that I didn't want to touch the guitar or piano in case I touched somebody's note. Somebody may own that note."

Despite their agreement on Klein, the former Beatles were now fairly disconnected socially, except for occasional business meetings (with Ono appearing on Lennon's behalf). Harrison found himself missing the old band. "[I]f John, Paul and Ringo get together in a room, I just hope they invite me along," he said in 1976. Three years later, when no such gatherings had happened, Harrison told one reporter he "was very interested to know whether John still writes tunes . . . or does he just forget all about music and not play guitar?" Shortly afterward, Harrison got his answer: Lennon and Ono were working on an album of all new songs, *Double Fantasy,* to be released in time for the Christmas season. And then, there was bad news: On the evening of December 8, 1980, a young man stepped from the shadows of the vestibule outside Lennon's apartment at New York City's Dakota building, called the singer's name and then fired four shots into his body. A short time later, Olivia Harrison was awakened by a call in the morning darkness, giving her the news. She woke Harrison and told him. "How bad is it?" he asked. "A flesh wound or something?" Olivia had to tell Harrison the truth about what four bullets at close range will accomplish: John Lennon, Harrison's childhood friend, was dead.

Harrison canceled his work for a while. He had been recording a new album, *Somewhere in England,* and he had also written a song called "All Those Years Ago," for Starr's next effort. With Starr's agreement, Harrison withdrew the song and rewrote its lyrics as a tribute to his dead friend's stature, and he recruited Starr and McCartney to add tracks to the revised tune. The song became an immediate hit in the U.S., but it was of little consolation to Harrison. "John's shooting definitely scared all of us–me, Paul and Ringo," Harrison is quoted as saying in Alan Clayson's biography, *George Harrison.* "When a fan recognizes me and rushes over, it definitely makes me nervous." After Lennon's murder, Harrison heightened the security around his home, Friar Park. He was determined that no unwelcome party would ever make his way past his estate's gates.

* ⋈ * ⋈ *

AFTER 'SOMEWHERE IN ENGLAND,' Harrison recorded two more studio albums, *Gone Troppo* in 1982 and *Cloud Nine* in 1987–though he was close to finishing another album shortly before his death. Jeff Lynne, the former leader of the heavily Beatles-influenced Electric Light Orchestra, worked on *Cloud Nine* with Harrison. The two discovered they shared a passion for an obscure James Ray song, "Got My Mind Set on You," and worked it up for a laugh. The result was another Number One single for Harrison. Shortly afterward, in the spring of 1988, a casual jam session attended by Harrison, Lynne, Tom Petty, Roy Orbison and Dylan in Dylan's garage in Malibu, California, flowered into a full-blown band, the only group that Harrison ever joined after the Beatles. The resulting album, *The Traveling Wilburys (Volume One),* was perhaps the craftiest and most joyful cooperative musical effort Harrison had participated in since *Rubber Soul* or *Revolver.* Harrison planned a series of Wilburys albums–perhaps even a movie–but then Roy Orbison died in December 1988. When Harrison, Dylan, Petty and Lynne gathered for an Orbison tribute to benefit Romanian orphans, they performed "Nobody's Child," a song that the Beatles used to play with Tony Sheridan in Hamburg, back in the early 1960s. The Wilburys made a second record in 1990, but without Orbison there was something lacking, and Harrison never regrouped the band.

In 1991, Harrison toured Japan with Eric Clapton and Clapton's band (released as *Live in Japan* in 1992). Part of the reason he went, he said, was that he had finally quit a lifetime of smoking and wanted some distraction and fresh air. In an October 1992 tribute concert to Dylan at Madison Square Garden, Harrison rendered startling versions of Dylan's "If Not for You" and "Absolutely Sweet Marie." He also turned up on occasional radio in-terviews, performing Dylan's "Every Grain of Sand," as well as versions of the Everly Brothers "Let It Be Me" and Pete Seeger's "The Bells of Rhymney." It was evident from these various performances that Harrison still had talent to burn whenever he chose to. But he rarely chose to. The consensus among some observers was that Harrison was scared of something. In the transcript of a 1996 conversation between Harrison and Swami Prabhupada, published in Giuliano's biography, Harrison said, "I feel a little animosity from people. In some ways the more committed you are, and the stronger you are in what you do, the stronger the animosity. Sometimes I get the feeling there's one person to whom it means something. . . ."

In the remainder of the 1990s, George Harrison's primary public activity was making peace with the Beatles, as people and as history. In 1989, when asked again if the band might still get back together, George Harrison stated, "As far as I'm concerned, there won't be a Beatles reunion as long as John Lennon remains dead." But in some ways a larger barrier was the relationship between Harrison and McCartney. McCartney had expressed interest in writing with Harrison, but Harrison expressed hurt that McCartney had waited so many years to make such an overture. Plus, both men freely admitted, they could simply grate on each other's nerves. Still, McCartney, Harrison and Starr had been long committed to *The Beatles Anthology* project, as a way of telling their own version of their history, releasing some previously unavailable tracks and reactivating their still commercially powerful recording catalogue. Yoko Ono gave the surviving Beatles two unfinished tracks by Lennon, "Free as a Bird" and "Real Love," to complete as they saw fit. Though Harrison would later somewhat disdain the new tracks, the final results sounded as if everybody involved worked sincerely and meticulously, and with "Free as a Bird" in particular, they even created something rather moving. "Whatever happened to/The life we once knew," McCartney sang in the song's middle part. "Can we really live/Without each other?" The song wasn't a statement about nostalgia but rather a commentary on all the chances and hopes, all the immeasurable possibilities that are lost when people who once loved each other cut themselves off from that communion. Not a bad or imprecise coda for what the Beatles did to themselves, and to their own history (and to their audience),

with their dissolution. And moments later, Harrison plays a guitar solo that sums up a quarter of a century of yearning and pain.

But there was more pain to come. In 1997, after beginning work on a new solo project, Harrison underwent surgery for throat cancer. The treatment was considered successful. At 3:00 a.m., December 30, 1999, Olivia Harrison was awakened by a loud crash at their Friar Park home. Her first thought was that a chandelier had fallen to the floor, but she couldn't be sure. She awoke her husband, who went downstairs to investigate. There, he felt a cold blast of air from a shattered window and smelled cigarette smoke. Harrison ran back upstairs and told Olivia to contact the grounds staff and call the police. Then Harrison saw a young man moving on the floor beneath him, carrying a lance that he had taken from a statue in Harrison's home. Harrison asked

him, "Who are you?" The man replied, "You know. Get down here." Harrison tackled the man, and the two rolled on the ground. The attacker began to stab at Harrison. Olivia rushed to join her husband and smashed the man in the head with a heavy table lamp. After a few blows, the man attacked Olivia and cut her head, then returned to Harrison, who had been stabbed severely in the chest and was fast growing weak. Harrison grabbed the attacker's knife by its blade just as local police rushed in and subdued the man. Harrison's lung was collapsed, and the blade had missed his heart by less than an inch. Harrison's son, Dhani, awakened by the commotion, rushed to his father's side. Both Dhani and the police noticed that Harrison was drifting out of consciousness, and they believed

Harrison and Olivia, in Italy, May 2001. Earlier that month, he had been treated for lung cancer at the Mayo Clinic in Rochester, Minnesota.

he was close to dying. "Oh, Dhani," Harrison said to his son, "I'm going out." As Harrison was taken away to an ambulance, Dhani called to him, "Dad! You are with me. . . . It's going to be okay." Harrison was moved off the serious list by the following afternoon.

The young man who attacked had a history of schizophrenia that had not been treated adequately. He told his lawyer, "The Beatles were witches," and that God had sent him to put Harrison to death. In the trial that followed, the jury found the attacker not guilty on the grounds of insanity, and the magistrate committed him to the psychiatric wing of a Merseyside hospital. He would be eligible for release if a mental health examiner board determined he was no longer a threat. Harrison and his family asked to be notified if he was released, but the judge denied their request.

Harrison's attack was followed by death threats, and he and his family considered leaving Friar Park. In the spring of 2001, Harrison underwent an operation to remove a cancerous growth on his lung. His lawyer reported that Harrison was in good spirits and that his prognosis was good. Harrison himself said, "I had a little throat cancer. I had a piece of my lung removed. And then I was almost murdered. But I seem to feel stronger." But throughout 2001 there were various reports of Harrison visiting hospitals in England and America in an effort to fight the cancer, which had now taken the form of a brain tumor. On Thursday, November 29, 2001, Harrison succumbed to the disease at 1:30 in the afternoon, reportedly at the Los Angeles home of Gavin de Becker, a friend of the family's and a security expert. Harrison had been in the city for two weeks, but his presence had been a well-guarded secret. "He left this world as he lived in it, conscious of God, fearless of death and at peace, surrounded by family and friends," the family announced in a statement. "He often said, 'Everything else can wait but the search for God cannot wait, and love one another.' "

✳ ⤙ ✳ ⤚ ✳

THE BEATLES' SECOND FEATURE FILM, *Help!*, contains a moment that is perhaps central to how the Beatles occupied the modern imagination. Near the beginning, a limousine arrives outside a row of London flats. The four Beatles disembark from the car, and George, John, Paul and Ringo each walk to separate doors of four flats, lined up alongside each other. The Beatles enter their seemingly independent residences, but once they're behind the doors we see that there are no walls between their apartments. They all live in one grand residence, outfitted with sunken beds, a Wurlitzer organ that rises from one corner of the floor, a strip of lawn, a library (largely full of John Lennon's writings) and a series of vending machines. At night, the Beatles sleep in beds sprawled across the room's interior. The message was: This is the Beatles' idealized home and playground—the dream dwelling where they lived as partners on common terms and in a shared quest, with no partitions dividing them.

It was an adroit and mocking insight into how countless fans viewed the Beatles in the 1960s: as the exemplars of a self-made family that might serve as a model of community for youth culture and popular music. In one way or another, this longing for community—the dream of self-willed equity and harmony in a world where familiar notions of family and accord were breaking down—would haunt rock's most meaningful moments in the 1960s. There's every indication that the Beatles themselves shared this dream—at least for a brief time. "We were tight," Harrison said in *The Beatles Anthology.* "I'll say that for us."

In 1983, though, Harrison reportedly told Geoffrey Giuliano, "All this stuff about the Beatles being able to save the world was rubbish. I can't even save myself." In a different conversation, with Swami Prabhupada, Harrison once said that there came a point in his meditations "where I can't relate to anyone anymore. . . . Not even . . . my friends, my wife, anybody!" Interesting remarks for a man who genuinely believed in ideals of love and unity, and yet who seemed to spend much of the last twenty-five or so years of his life keeping a wary distance from the world.

There is no question that Harrison's devotion to Indian teachings and spiritual precepts was sincere, even if he did not always stay with the disciplines that Hindu beliefs demanded—the most interesting spiritual seekers tend to be the ones who are wise enough (or simply human enough) to wander off course periodically, turning their searches into enduring struggles. For Harrison, Hinduism—and the teachings of Swami Prabhupada, Paramahansa Yogananda and Maharishi Mahesh Yogi, who were truly keen and even

droll philosophers—may have fulfilled some deeper void that he had moved through his entire life, and that his experience with the Beatles only deepened, rather than resolved.

Like all the Beatles, Harrison was not only the object of intense love, but he believed that acting with a will and devotion to love was among the highest purposes of life. But Harrison also understood that in the end, you likely need a lot more than love to make it through this world or redeem your pain. Sometimes

November 30, 2001, the day after Harrison's death, fans around the world gathered to pay their respects. This memorial was displayed on the Hollywood Walk of Fame in Los Angeles.

darkness is irrefutable, and sometimes love and understanding can't save a troubled heart or a soul in harm's way—which was the subject of one of Harrison's best songs, "The Art of Dying." Or, to put it differently: Love is a wonderful thing, but love can also be a costly and terrible thing.

Few love stories in the twentieth century better illustrated that dichotomy than the journey of the Beatles. I suspect that nobody else in that group carried that knowledge with greater weight, yearning or honor than George Harrison. We have had few people like him in the history of the popular arts, and we are richer for the time that he lived with us.　　❋

A Life

IN
PHOTOS

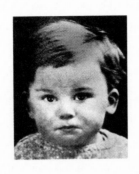

George Harrison, born February 25, 1943

Photographs by

JÜRGEN VOLLMER

ASTRID KIRCHHERR

MAX SCHELER

HARRY BENSON

DAVID HURN

P.J. GRIFFITHS

CURT GUNTHER

HENRY GROSSMAN

MARK SELIGER

Text by

JENNY ELISCU

1961–1970

Growing Up With the Beatles

JÜRGEN VOLLMER

In 1961, Jürgen Vollmer brought a teenage George Harrison to a lake in Hamburg to photograph the guitarist by himself. The Beatles had returned to Germany for a second stint at the city's seedy, red-light-district clubs—an experience Harrison referred to as his only "higher education."

E WAS SUCH A SWEET and charming little boy," says German photographer Jürgen Vollmer, speaking about George Harrison, whom he photographed when the Beatles came to Hamburg in 1961. "But he also had this melancholy feeling that I identified with. I didn't have much contact with Paul, and I was always a

little afraid of John because he could be arrogant and overly ironic. But George didn't have a mean streak in him."

Vollmer had been going with friends Astrid Kirchherr and Klaus Voormann to see the band play at the Kaiserkeller and the Top Ten–two seedy Hamburg clubs located in the city's red-light district. "It smelled like sex," he says, describing the clubs' atmosphere. "The Beatles were playing really hard American rock & roll, and there was all of this sexual energy and tension in the crowd. That's why I went night after night."

The Beatles would play alternating hour-long sets with bands including Rory Storm and the Hurricanes and Gerry and the Pacemakers. "They were taking uppers to maintain their energy; it was incredible," Vollmer says. "The crowd was very rough, but they were usually well received."

During their stint at the Top Ten, the Beatles lived in an apartment directly above the club's dance floor. Vollmer had already photographed the band outdoors but wanted to shoot them in the club, as well. Harrison suggested that Vollmer come by during the day, when the Top Ten was closed. "I didn't have a flash; I didn't know how to use one," he says. "So I took every lamp in the place and put it near the stage, and they played for me while I took pictures."   ☀

"When I first saw the Beatles," said Vollmer, "I thought they were real rough 'n' tough rockers. They looked just like their audience. But when I met them I realized that it was all an act."

Photograph by **JÜRGEN VOLLMER**

The Beatles arrived back in Hamburg, Germany, to play the Star-Club the day after Sutcliffe's death. Kirchherr photographed Lennon and Harrison in the attic Sutcliffe had used as a painting studio. "That's the first time I noticed how strong George was, to comfort John in that bad time after Stu's death," she said. "He doesn't look like an eighteen-year-old boy. There was so much more in his eyes."

STRID KIRCHHERR, whose photos document the Beatles' earliest days, was an art-school student in Germany when she met the group in 1960. While the band was playing a residency at Hamburg's Kaiserkeller club that year, Kirchherr's boyfriend, artist Klaus Voormann, stumbled into a Beatles show. He was blown away and dragged Kirchherr back with him. "It's very hard to remember much about that first visit, because at the time I didn't know that it was going to change my life," Kirchherr wrote in *Hamburg Days,* a limited-edition 1999 collection of her Beatles photographs. "For me, it was a visual thing. I couldn't believe it."

With the little English she spoke, she asked the members of the band–John Lennon, Paul McCartney, George Harrison, drummer Pete Best and bassist Stuart Sutcliffe–if she could photograph them. "We loved the idea," Harrison said. "It was something that was going to help us get publicity. We'd never seen such fantastic photography. In those pictures, we looked so cool."

Though Kirchherr was smitten with Sutcliffe, she became close friends with Harrison–she was five years older but considered him her big brother. "George was lovely," she once said. "Wide-eyed, innocent, open and very loving and warm. He used to tell me that he'd never met a girl like me before, and he meant it. I felt protective of George. He was a long way from home and seemed to miss the attention of his family." Kirchherr remained friends with Harrison until his death.

Kirchherr was an impressive young woman: a beautiful artist with her own car and her own style– an unconventional cropped hairdo and a wardrobe dominated by black boyish clothes. She is credited not only with influencing the way the Beatles dressed (having persuaded Sutcliffe to trade his teddy-boy attire for leather pants and a collarless Pierre Cardin-style jacket) but also with inspiring them to cut their ducktail coifs into the famous rounded shags.

Kirchherr, who continued taking pictures through the Eighties and still lives in Hamburg, began dating Sutcliffe a couple of weeks after meeting the band. By 1961 they were engaged; less than a year later, Sutcliffe died suddenly of a brain hemorrhage, on April 10, 1962. The relationship was documented in the 1993 film *Backbeat.* ❦

Photograph by **ASTRID KIRCHHERR**

Kirchherr's first photos of the Beatles were shot at the Hamburg, Germany, fairgrounds. Original Beatles Pete Best, Harrison, Lennon, McCartney and Stuart Sutcliffe (from left) stood in front of a trailer used to transport roller coasters. Lennon had just acquired a new Rickenbacker guitar; the left-handed McCartney posed holding Lennon's old guitar, upside down.

Astrid was totally responsible for our whole image. She said, 'Hold your head here, turn to the left.' . . . All we did was pose.

—GEORGE HARRISON

Working on a scene for 'A Hard Day's Night,' filmed at London's Twickenham Studios during the spring of 1964

MAX SCHELER

HEN MAX SCHELER arrived in London to photograph the Beatles in February 1964, Beatlemania was in full bloom. During the previous three weeks, the band had performed on *The Ed Sullivan Show* twice, played at New York's Carnegie Hall and scored their fifth Number One song, "Can't Buy Me Love." Scheler, on assignment for the German news magazine *Stern,* joined the Beatles during the filming of *A Hard Day's Night* and traveled with them on the train where a portion of the film was shot. It was there that George Harrison met his first wife, Pattie Boyd, who played a schoolgirl in the movie. At night, Scheler says, "George would strum on his guitar, and Astrid [Kirchherr] would dance with Ringo. . . . George was more approachable than the others. John seemed very sarcastic; Ringo was a bit hard; Paul was the diplomat; and George, well, he was just this pretty boy. I liked him a great deal." ❧

63

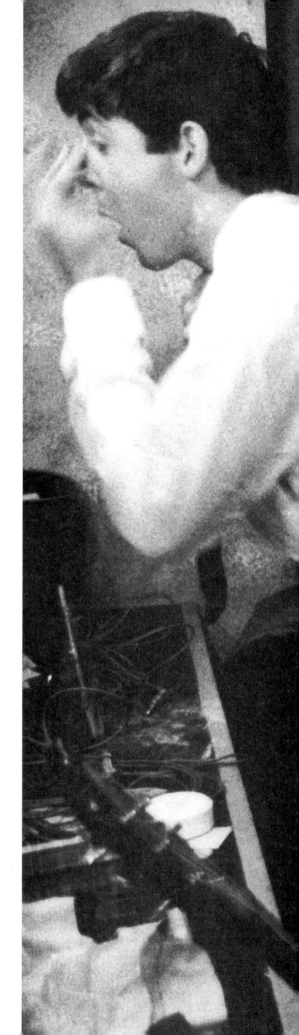

P.J. GRIFFITHS

IVERPOOL WAS a very vibrant place at the time," says P.J. Griffiths, who shot the Beatles on three separate occasions during the early Sixties. "You hung around with the right wrong crowd and got friendly with various musicians. You were never sure who was going to make it."

Griffiths was introduced to the Beatles by his best friend, Adrian Henri, who was in a band with Paul McCartney's brother Michael. "McCartney's brother would vouch for me as being okay," he says. "I hung out like a pal. I didn't show up with an assistant and lights. I just wish at the time I'd realized they were going to be as famous as they became. I regret that I didn't spend more time around them."

Griffiths' most vivid memory of his time with the Beatles is watching them read the fan mail that poured into their dressing room. "John's going, 'Jesus Christ, she doesn't really think I would do that with her, does she?'" he says. "It was incredible stuff like, 'I want to sit on your guitar while you put your tongue down my . . .' These Liverpool girls, they were the best."

Getting dressed at Liverpool's Empire Theatre. "They were local boys made good, putting on a big show," says Griffiths.

Photograph by **P.J. GRIFFITHS**

In Amsterdam, the Beatles' 1964 tour got off to a bumpy start: For three shows in the Netherlands and Denmark, the band hired a drummer to fill in for Ringo Starr, who was ill.

HARRY BENSON

HOTOGRAPHING THE BEATLES' first world tour in 1964, Harry Benson witnessed not only the band's public high points–performing on *The Ed Sullivan Show,* meeting Muhammad Ali–but also private moments when the four were just hanging out in hotel suites, opening fan mail, writing music and goofing off. Benson snapped some of today's most instantly recognizable images of the band, including a legendary shot of them in their pajamas, walloping one another with pillows. That particular night he had waited up with the band until 3:00 a.m., when they received news from manager Brian Epstein that "I Want to Hold Your Hand" had reached Number One in America. He also traveled with them from London to Amsterdam and Paris as well as to the States. He spent much of his free time with George Harrison, visiting nightclubs and talking in the guitarist's hotel room.

"George used to say he never expected to make any money with the band–just enough to open a little business," Benson wrote in his memoir, *The Beatles: In the Beginning*. "Six, seven months,

Above: While his band mates were exploring New York, Harrison, who was sick, stayed in his suite at the Plaza Hotel, reading get-well telegrams and lounging in silk pajamas he had received as a gift. His sister, Louise, helped nurse him back to health in time for the Beatles' U.S. debut on 'The Ed Sullivan Show.'

that's what he thought it would be, because rock groups come and go so quickly. [He] had bought a Jaguar XK-140 and was hoping that he would be able to make enough money to keep it, maybe by doing shows himself."

In 1966, Benson joined the Beatles on the road for their third—and final—world tour. "Once they stopped touring, I didn't photograph them as a group anymore," he said. "They had clearly gone on to other lifestyles, and I went on as well." ⚜

Photographs by **HARRY BENSON**

On tour that year, it was crazy. Not within the band. In the band we were normal, and the rest of the world was crazy.

—GEORGE HARRISON

"They needed to let off steam," Benson said, describing the inspiration for his most famous Beatles shot.

Photograph by **HARRY BENSON**

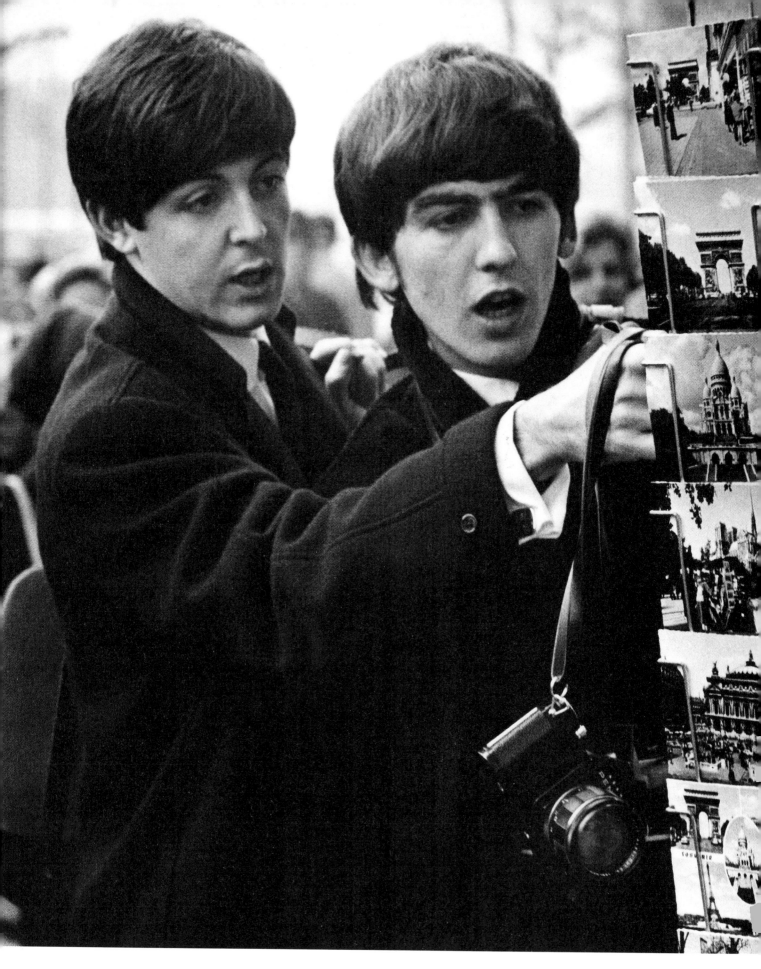

Photograph by **HARRY BENSON**

"It was a cold day for sightseeing,
but we went anyway," Benson
said, recalling a day trolling
along the Champs-Elysées during
the band's visit to Paris in the
winter of 1964. For three weeks,
they played almost nightly
at the Olympia Theater and then
retired to their suites at the
posh George V Hotel. According
to Benson, "They liked playing
tourist. They all had cameras
and liked taking pictures, even if
it was only of each other."

Photograph by **HARRY BENSON**

All these people were clamoring to meet us—like Muhammad Ali. It was all part of being a Beatle, getting lugged around and thrust into rooms full of pressmen. Ali was quite cute, really.

—GEORGE HARRISON

While visiting Miami Beach to make their second 'Ed Sullivan' appearance, Benson took the Beatles to meet a young fighter known then as Cassius Clay. Clay toyed with the group, calling McCartney "the pretty one," but adding, "You're not as pretty as I am."

WHILE THE BEATLES were filming *A Hard Day's Night* in 1964, David Hurn spent ten days with the group, photographing them for publicity stills. "[Director] Dick Lester asked me to come and do what they laughingly call 'special photography,' " Hurn remembers. "You arrive being friends with the director and feel you'll have access to do what you want to do. And then you realize that in the minds of everyone else on the set, you're in the way." In addition to being a respected photojournalist during the Sixties, Hurn shot movie posters and stills for the first five James Bond flicks, *Barbarella* and the Beatles' second film, *Help!* He got along best with Ringo Starr and recalls that George Harrison was "exceedingly shy." Yet it was the guitarist whose life Hurn ultimately impacted

On the set of 'A Hard Day's Night,' 1964. "The Beatles were loved by everyone's mothers," says Hurn. "They were good scrubbed lads in suits, quiet and not riotous like some other groups."

most: The thirty-year-old photographer introduced Harrison to his future wife, Pattie Boyd. At the time, Hurn's friend, a fellow photographer named Eric Swain, was dating Boyd. "He was quite proud of her," Hurn says, "and sort of paraded her, like a little dog." Boyd wanted to meet the Beatles, so Hurn convinced Lester to let her be an extra in the film. "I introduced her to them all," Hurn explains. "I had no idea that the one had googled at her more than the others. Of course, I wasn't the greatest friend of dear Eric Swain from then."   ❈

"The Beatles were very conscious that being free and easy was part of their image," said 'A Hard Day's Night' director Dick Lester. "What fan wants to be told that her idols work ten hours a day?"

The Beatles were the first to give confidence to the youth of England. They sent the class thing sky-high.

—*A HARD DAY'S NIGHT* DIRECTOR DICK LESTER

Photograph by **DAVID HURN**

Our original intention was just to be in a band as opposed to having a job. The goals were quite small, really.

—GEORGE HARRISON

The Beatles played twenty-five dates during the 1964 North American tour. Opening acts included the Righteous Brothers and Jackie DeShannon.

Photograph by CURT GUNTHER

CURT GUNTHER

HE BEATLES did not have a large entourage traveling with them during their 1964 world tour, and members of the press were generally not welcome on the band's chartered American Flyers Airlines Lockheed Electra. It was only because of his persistence and his sterling reputation that photojournalist Curt Gunther was ultimately allowed on board. While traveling with the Beatles, Gunther documented their rare quiet moments and the hysteria that followed them around North America. The photographer passed away in 1991, but in *Fifty Years Adrift,* the Beatles' former press agent Derek Taylor remembered, "Every day Curt Gunther, drawing deeply on a mentholated cigarette, his wise and cunning old eyes boring into mine, would say, 'Derek, we gotta have some special pictures, something original.'" When the band visited a Missouri ranch, Gunther found an old wood-and-iron door that he considered the perfect backdrop. Taylor wrote: "'There she is,' he said of the setup. 'That's the picture I want to make. Then I die happy.'"

"In 1964, we seemed to fit a week into every day," Harrison said. "I didn't think beyond the moment during that U.S. trip. I thought, 'We'll enjoy what's happening and go out there and do our thing.' " The guitarist warms up with John Lennon in a backstage bathroom.

Photograph by **CURT GUNTHER**

The Beatles performed at New York's Shea Stadium before a crowd of forty-three thousand people on August 23, 1966.

Opposite: In the mid-Sixties, Harrison said, "We were going all the time. It was always hit-and-run." This page: Poolside at the Deauville Hotel in Miami Beach, Florida, February 1964. The band's second 'Ed Sullivan Show' appearance was filmed in the hotel's Mau Mau Club.

This page, right: An extremely Day-Glo "All You Need Is Love" recording session. Below: The Beatles as Sgt. Pepper's Lonely Hearts Club Band, 1967. Opposite, top: A vacationing Harrison, singing "Baby You're a Rich Man," attracts a parade of flower children at San Francisco's Golden Gate Park, August 1967. Bottom: In Rishikesh, India, January 1968. Harrison spent ten days composing, arranging and recording music for the film 'Wonderwall.'

The Beatles and their wives, with Maharishi Mahesh Yogi at his ashram in Rishikesh, India, in early 1968. It was Harrison's wife, Pattie Boyd, who introduced the band to the maharishi's teachings on Transcendental Meditation.

At a press conference for the release of the 'George Harrison' album in 1979. "People who truly live a life in music are telling the world, 'Forget the bad parts. Just take the music, the goodness.'"

1971–1979 } *The Solo Years*

HENRY GROSSMAN

EORGE WAS GROWING," says Henry Grossman of Harrison's 1974 U.S. solo tour. "The audience was growing, too. George was a bit ahead of them at that point." The performances—launched following the release of his fifth solo album, *Dark Horse*—were often criticized for favoring new, jazzier material and Indian music over

Beatles tunes. When he did play oldies, he playfully changed lyrics on songs such as "Something," about his ex-wife, Pattie Boyd: "There's something in the way/Try and remove it, nicely though, find yourself some other lover."

Grossman, who photographed the Beatles extensively in the mid-Sixties for *Time, Life* and the *London Daily Mirror,* notes that morale on the tour was high. "You can see it, looking at the photos of the band arm in arm," he says. "They were making music, that's what it was about."

Harrison had personally invited his old friend Grossman to shoot the *Dark Horse* tour. "I knocked on the door of the rehearsal studio in Los Angeles," Grossman remembers. "When George opened the door, he gave me a big hug. We were like brothers at that point."

For a string of West Coast dates, the photographer traveled on a private jet crowded with musicians including former Beatles sideman Billy Preston, saxophonist Tom Scott and a fifteen-piece Indian orchestra, led by Ravi Shankar. "George subliminally valued things," Grossman says. "He was in touch with a deeper reality. It was in his nature to be an artist. What George saw, he put into music." ※

Above: With future wife Olivia Arias. Opposite, top: "It was always like we were going to a party when we got on the plane," Grossman remembers. The band was briefly joined by actor Peter Sellers (between Shankar and Harrison). Bottom: "I'll play with Billy Preston whenever I have the opportunity. He has so much energy."

Photographs by HENRY GROSSMAN

"Why live in the darkness all your life? If you are unhappy, look for the light within.

—GEORGE HARRISON

Harrison and Olivia Arias, at a California hotel in 1975. Three years later, the couple—already parents to a one-month-old Dhani— married on September 2, 1978.

Photographs by **HENRY GROSSMAN**

This page, clockwise from top left: A 1969 portrait; "The first real strength I ever met is Ravi Shankar, this little guy," Harrison said in 1974; on the set of 'The Dick Cavett Show,' November 1971; album photo session for 'All Things Must Pass,' 1970; with his father and brother in 1974. Opposite: Performing with Ravi Shankar in May 1997 on VH1's 'Hard Rock Live.'

George's passion for all the music he loved and the serious quest for religion always amazed me.

—RAVI SHANKAR

MARK SELIGER

*T*HE SHOOT almost didn't take place," photographer Mark Seliger says of George Harrison's session for ROLLING STONE's twenty-fifth anniversary issue, in 1992. According to Seliger, Harrison had been reluctant to participate: He was still upset about the pan his album *Dark Horse* had received in the magazine eighteen

Photograph by **MARK SELIGER**

years earlier. "I had just shot Tom Petty, and he said, 'If you really want to get on George's good side, have a couple of nice ukuleles there,' " Seliger says. "For the third setup, we photographed him with the ukulele. After the last shot, he started playing these Hawaiian ballads, song after song, for twenty minutes straight. The entire entourage just sat there–it was the Beatles voice on these quirky little Hawaiian songs! It was nothing you'd ever heard before, but strangely familiar–one of those rare, poignant times as a photographer when you meet greatness."

I'm not really a career person. I'm a gardener, basically.

—GEORGE HARRISON, 2000

"I have serious moments," Harrison said in 1987. "But I never lost a sense of humor."

This page, right: Vacationing with his second wife, Olivia. Below: On the grounds of his Friar Park estate, 1987. "It's like Disneyland," Harrison said. Opposite, clockwise from top: At home with Olivia; Grand Prix enthusiast Harrison, at the races with Dhani; a family portrait, 1987: "With a child around," Harrison said, "I can realize what it was like to be my father. At the same time, you can relive certain aspects of being a child. It somehow completes this generation thing."

This page, clockwise from top: With fellow Traveling Wilburys Jeff Lynne (left) and Tom Petty in 1988; Harrison was the surprise guest at a 1992 tribute to late Toto drummer Jeff Porcaro that also featured Eddie Van Halen (left); partying with Ringo at Los Angeles' Bar One in 1990; with the Rolling Stones' Ron Wood, performing at a 1992 Bob Dylan tribute concert. Opposite: At Friar Park, 1987.

By Nick Jones

RS 5 & 6 ∗ FEBRUARY 1968

1968

An Early Interview

WITH GEORGE

The Maharishi and the meaning of Sgt. Pepper

The Maharishi Mahesh Yogi is being criticized, as are the Beatles, in connection with your studies in Transcendental Meditation.

It's easier to criticize somebody than to see yourself. We had got to the point where we were looking for somebody like the maharishi, and then there he was. It's been about three years of thinking, looking for why we're here—the purpose of what we're doing here on this world, getting born and dying. Normally people don't think about it, and then they just die—and then they've gone and missed it—because we do come here for some

purpose. And I've found out that the reason we come here is to get back to that thing God had, whatever you might call God—you know, that scene.

Then the music, Indian music, just seemed to have something very spiritual for me, and it became a stepping-stone for me to find out about other things. Finding out all about Hinduism and all those sort of religions made me realize that every religion is just the same scene, really.

You're taught to just have faith, you don't have to worry about it, just believe what we're telling you. And

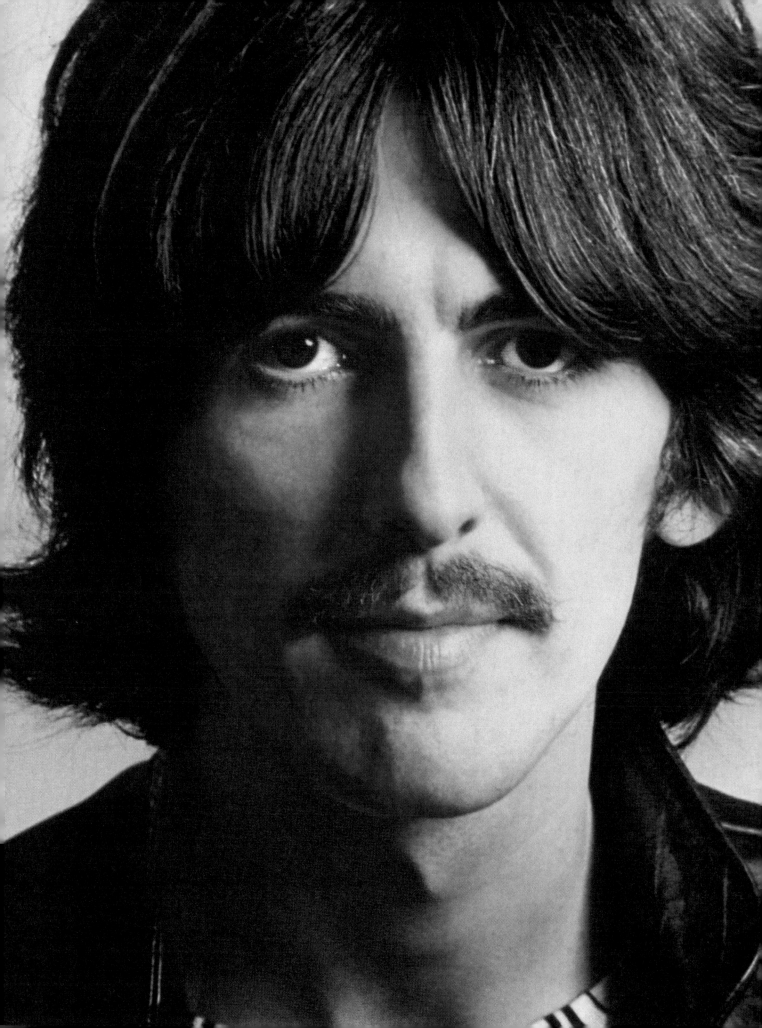

this is what makes the Indian one such a groove for me, and I'm sure for a lot of other people. Because over there they say, "Don't believe in anything . . . if there's a god we must see him, if there's a soul we must perceive it," and so on.

It's better to be an outspoken atheist than a hypocrite, so their whole teaching is, Don't believe in nothing until you've witnessed it for yourself. I really feel and believe in this whole sort of scene—you know, God. When you say the word *God* people are going to curl up and cringe—they all interpret it in a different way.

How do these realizations fit into your everyday life?

Everybody lives their lives thinking this is reality and then say to people like us, "Oh, you're just escaping from reality." They seriously term this scene—of waking up, going out to work, going home again, go-

Previous page: Harrison's portrait from the White Album. Above: A contemplative moment in '68. Opposite: A July 1968 shoot, when the band was recording the White Album.

ing to sleep, dreaming, waking up again, and all that— reality! But in actual fact you're into illusion—it's nothing to do with reality, because reality is God alone. Everything else is just an illusion.

I don't like to use the word *religious,* but when you get into that scene, when you go through yoga and meditation, it's just . . . self-realization. That's the whole thing why people have missed God. They haven't been able to see God because he is hidden in themselves.

How important do you think positive music is in this huge evolutionary cycle?

Very important. I think there is spiritual music. This is why I'm so hung up on Indian music, and from the day I got into it till the day I die, I still believe it's the greatest music ever on our level of existence. I've learned a hell of a lot about Hinduism from being in India, things I've read and from Ravi Shankar, who's really too much. So great. Not only in his music but in him, as well. This is the thing: He is the music, and the music is him, the whole culture of the Indian philosophy.

Mainly it's this thing of discipline. Discipline is something that we don't like–especially young people, where they have to go through school, and they put you in the army, and all that discipline. But in a different way I've found out it's very important, because the only way those musicians are great is because they've been disciplined by their guru or teacher, and they've surrendered themselves to the person they want to be. It's only by complete surrender and doing what that bloke tells you that you're going to get there, too. So with their music they do just that. You must practice twelve hours a day for years and years. Shankar has studied every part of the music until he improvises the music and it is just him, he is the music.

Was this the point you were trying to make in your ads that said, "Sergeant Pepper IS the Beatles"?

I feel this is something we've been trying to do all the time–keep that identification with people. It gets harder and harder the more famous you get. People see you, they put you up on that pedestal, and they really believe you're different from them. With Sergeant Pepper we've always tried to keep this identification and tried to do things for those people, to please those people, because in actual fact, they're us, too, really.

But at the same time, we're all responsible in a way because we're influencing a lot of people, so really, it's to influence them in the right way.

A lot of people, though, never realize what you're giving them.

Well, lots of people do, but then there's always the other ones who write in saying, "Why the fuck do you think you are doing that?" The maharishi says this level that we're on is like the surface of the ocean, which is always changing, chopping and changing, and we're living on the surface with these waves crashing about. But unless we're anchored on the bottom we're at the mercy of whatever goes on on the surface. So you go into meditation and your thoughts get smaller all the time, finer and finer, until you get right down there, until that's just pure consciousness, and you anchor yourself to that– and once you've established that anchor then it doesn't matter what goes on up on the surface. ❁

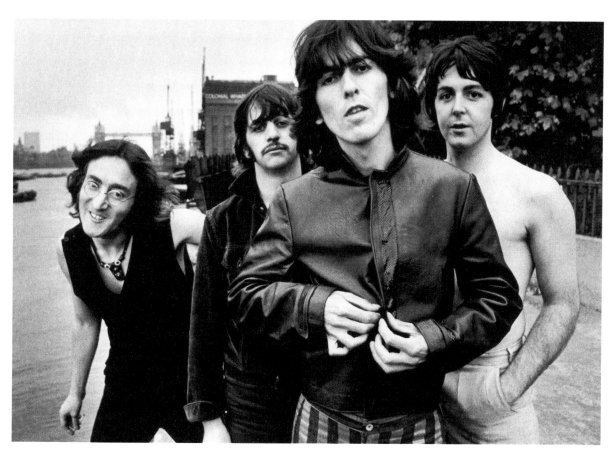

THE CONCERT FOR Bangladesh

The birth of rock charity

I<small>T WASN'T ONLY THE GLAMOUR</small> of the event that made it memorable, or the brilliance of the music, or even the impossible pantheon gathered onstage. It was more than that: The George Harrison benefit for the starving children of Bangladesh was a brief, incandescent revival of all that was best about the Sixties.

By now it is a cliché to say that Dylan and the Beatles constructed important myths of the last decade and, more than anyone else, helped us toward a common cultural vision. Now the things they sang about—love, peace and the courage to explore our own minds—so often seem to have passed into suspension.

The Harrison concert marked, even if only briefly, a rediscovery of those old concerns. Dylan sang "A Hard Rain's A-Gonna Fall," and it seemed the more chilling for the passage of years since he sang it last. Harrison performed his new single, "Bangla-Desh"–proceeds from which will also go to the refugees from East Pakistan. In a way, these two men reasserted themselves as leaders in music and regained for it some of its moral stature.

Featuring Harrison with Bob Dylan, Eric Clapton, Ringo Starr and others, the concert generated twelve million dollars.

The concert was great. In fact, there were two concerts, on the afternoon and evening of Sunday, August 1, each before a sellout crowd of more than twenty thousand in Madison Square Garden. The performances were nearly identical, the evening's perhaps slightly more lustrous.

It opened with Ravi Shankar and one of India's finest sarod players, Ali Akbar Khan, backed by Alla Rakha on tabla. Seated on a richly colored rug, they performed a beautiful evening raga, moving swiftly to the fast sections as an accommodation to the audience, then improvised an exciting duet based on a folk tune from East Pakistan. With his incense, his yellow flowers to either side of the stage and the beauty of his music, Shankar calmed the audience and then offered a preview of the hard rhythm to come as he and Khan exchanged and imitated each other's energetic riffs. Ravi Shankar had conceived of the concert, and he lent it enormous dignity.

During the intermission between raga and rock, they screened a disturbing film about the Pakistani refugees: It showed crows picking at carrion, children bloated with malnutrition, the dead and dying victims of cholera.

As the stage was reset in darkness, the anticipation of the audience swelled audibly. A surprisingly young crowd was seated in a huge horseshoe sweeping around the stage set up at the west end of the Garden. The silhouettes of the musicians entering the stage area blotted out some of the red amplifier lights, the applause began, the first loud notes of Harrison's "Wah-Wah" came rolling out of the darkness, the spotlights switched on, and there was Harrison in a white suit and burnt orange shirt, surrounded by an ocean of musicians.

The band was so strong during "Wah-Wah" that Harrison's voice barely cut through. No wonder: Eric Clapton, in a Levi shirt, jacket and jeans, stood to Harrison's left, churning out wah-wahs. Leon Russell was flailing the piano just behind Clapton. Ringo Starr—Ringo!—and Jim Keltner of Joe Cocker fame were behind the two sets of drums. Billy Preston sat at the organ to Harrison's right, where Jesse Davis (formerly with Taj Mahal and now on his own) worked on another guitar and Klaus Voormann, who did the extraordinary bass on Harrison's and John Lennon's albums, picked away.

And on one side of the stage, four members of Badfinger, whose *No Dice* album Harrison had produced, amiably strummed acoustic guitars that no one could quite hear. Next to them were seven horns under the di-

rection of Jim Horn from California. And on the other side, behind Preston and his Hammond B-3, was a nine-voice choir. Harrison vamped on his white solid-body guitar and anxiously looked around to see if the whole ship was getting off all right. He seemed nervous—"Just thinking about it makes me shake," he said beforehand—but everything sounded fine. It was the biggest, largest rock band—better yet, rock orchestra—ever put together.

One night only!

Without a pause, they went into "My Sweet Lord." The opening was engulfed by a classic two-part applause pattern—a swarm of cheers from aficionados picking up on the first couple of notes, then a heavier barrage on the opening words from the folks more into Top Forty radio. Harrison's voice sounded confident and more relaxed than at the first show: He now sang trills around the notes, rocked from foot to foot and seemed to be enjoying himself. The choral hallelujahs were handled nicely by the consort of rockers extending off into indefinite shadow.

* * *

THE LIGHTS WENT DOWN for a minute. Leon Russell suddenly appeared and plugged in his bass. Harrison picked up an electric guitar and slipped a steel slide around his finger. Ringo Starr appeared from the side with a tambourine in hand. The stage remained unlit.

A short man with fuzzy hair and a denim jacket hovered near the amps to the right of the stage. Harrison stepped to the microphone and said, "I'd like to bring on a friend of us all, Mr. Bob Dylan."

So there he was, in baggy brown pants and a green T-shirt, toting a D-size Martin, the old harmonica holder around his neck. He stood smiling slightly during the prolonged ovation, licked his lips, began strumming, stepped to the mike and sang "A Hard Rain's A-Gonna Fall." He sounded better than he ever has, his voice lean, cutting and under perfect control. He stood almost bowlegged, unwinding each line, then leaning back from the mike and ducking behind the harmonica without blowing a note.

He didn't actually play the harp until the middle of his next song, "It Takes a Lot to Laugh, It Takes a Train to Cry." His harmonica playing ran along the old edges of sadness, discord and suspense. Harrison played a light, quiet bottleneck guitar, and altogether it amounted to probably the finest version ever of a splendid song.

Without a word, Dylan went into "Blowin' in the Wind." In the dressing room with Harrison before the concert Dylan had done some new songs, but onstage he ventured nothing more recent than 1966, and so, people were offered another Dylan puzzle to contemplate.

After "Just Like a Woman," the lights came on. Dylan looked around hesitantly, held up both fists like a strongman, grinned and then strode offstage.

Next, the score of musicians returned to their places onstage and Harrison spoke into the mike: "It's really hard to follow Bob." And then Harrison hit the opening lick of "Something," and the show was off to yet another peak, another performance that seemed to defy history. It closed the show.

For his encore, Harrison chose his new single, "Bangla-Desh":

> My friend came to me with sadness in his eyes
> Told me that he wanted help
> Before his country dies;
> Although I couldn't feel the pain
> I knew I had to try.
> Now I'm asking all of you
> To help us save some lives
> Bangladesh, Bangladesh

* * *

BANGLADESH" means "Bengal nation"–the name taken by secessionists in East Pakistan. In recent months, East Pakistan has become a lightning rod for misery; the very fact that it took something like the Harrison concert to awaken many in America to the suffering in East Pakistan is an indication of how compassion dwindles with distance.

A cyclone struck Bangladesh last November and killed five hundred thousand people–a figure impossible to understand. Then, as if to conspire with nature, the Pakistani army launched against the people of the east one of the most brutal military slaughters in modern history, machine-gunning crowds of civilians, destroying whole villages and putting the torch to the dense slums of Dacca, East Pakistan's largest city. In the four months since that campaign began, by the most conservative estimates, a quarter of a million people

have been killed, possibly many more.

The suggestion that George Harrison do a benefit for these people came from an Indian whose father was born in East Pakistan: Ravi Shankar.

"I was very much concerned," Shankar said at his hotel the day after the concert. "I was asked by many different societies to give some benefit performances to raise some funds. . . . So I thought of getting a big performer, a big show and getting a minimum of fifty thousand dollars, and I just asked George. He was very moved, he felt very deeply, and he said, 'Yes, I think I'll be able to do something.' "

That was six weeks before the concert, and then Harrison became the prime mover, gathering the musicians, making the phone calls, getting the commitments and setting up the show. He had immediately called his manager, Allen Klein, who acted as producer, and got Madison Square Garden booked, and he called Bob Dylan, who said he was "interested."

Badfinger flew into New York from London on the Monday before the concert, followed by the horn players. Harrison wrote arrangements for them and began rehearsals. Starr arrived Thursday. Finally Dylan showed up at Harrison's hotel room Saturday morning, played a few songs and said he'd do it. Harrison had phoned Paul McCartney and asked him to play, but he said no. John Lennon stopped in New York a couple of days earlier but went home to attend to the legal battles he and Yoko Ono are fighting for custody of her child. Mick Jagger, recording at the Stones' camp in the south of France, tried to make it but couldn't get a visa.

The event itself was simply one of the great rock concerts. Harrison had insisted that he wanted to do a solid, professional show rather than some kind of superjam, and it worked. The audience responded with exceptional warmth and respect, listening intently and exploding into applause when the music ended.

"They were so happy, the joy of their being there was felt by each of us," Shankar said. "This hasn't happened for so long now. Since Woodstock I have been to about five or six rock festivals–the last one was three months ago, and I promised myself never again, because there is no more flower child and love but only violence and drugs."   ✻

By Ben Fong-Torres

RS 176 ✦ DECEMBER 19, 1974

1974

THE TROUBLED

U.S. Tour

A new band, but fans still wanted the Beatles

HOLY KRISHNA! What kind of an opening night for George Harrison is *this*? Ravi Shankar asks for silence and no smoking during his music. Silence is very important, he says, because music is eternal, and out of the silence comes the music. Something like that. But, instead, out of the audience comes this piercing death cry, followed by a rain of war whoops. After a few minutes people start shouting, "Get funky!" and "Rock & roll!"

Harrison, meantime, is hoarse from the beginning and strains through each song. Billy Preston eventually perks up the show with two numbers in the second half, but the night ends with more Indian music and more cries for rock & roll. He performs "My Sweet Lord," and out of the silence comes the silence–a still and seated audience with only the front section clapping along.

* * *

"I realize the Beatles did fill a space in the Sixties, and all the people who the Beatles meant something to have grown up. It's like with anything. You grow up

with it and you get attached to it. That's one of the problems in our lives, becoming too attached to things. But I understand the Beatles in many ways did nice things, and it's appreciated, the people still like them. The problem comes when they want to live in the past, and they want to hold onto something and are afraid of change."

—GEORGE HARRISON at his Los Angeles press conference, October 23, 1974

* * *

THE LAST TIME I saw George Harrison in the flesh as a Beatle, he was a standout. The group was on a stage covering second base at Candlestick Park, home of the San Francisco Giants, the night of August 29, 1966. San Francisco was the last stop of a nineteen-city American tour. JPG and R, all in white shirts and Mod green jackets that matched the outfield grass, had strolled out of the first-base dugout, waving casually at a mad crowd of twenty-six thousand, and laughed through eleven songs in thirty minutes flat.

And I remember how Harrison stood out from the other three that evening. He wore white socks.

As things turned out, the Candlestick Park show was the last concert the Beatles ever did. "We got in a rut," Harrison told Hunter Davies, the biographer, years later. "It was just a bloody big row. Nobody could hear. We got worse as musicians, playing the same old junk every day. There was no satisfaction at all."

The next month, Harrison and his then-wife, Pattie Boyd, were off to India. It was five more years before Harrison returned to the stage, at the behest of Shankar and for the benefit of the people of Bangladesh, East Pakistan. He was the host, dressed all in white, gathering such friends as Preston, Ringo Starr, Eric Clapton, Leon Russell and Bob Dylan around him. And it was there, at Madison Square Garden, that Harrison tasted the desire to tour again.

"He was definitely inspired after Bangladesh," said Preston. "He wanted to do it again, right away. But it took some time. Bangladesh was an exceptional show because everybody was there. He had to do a lot of thinking on this one, because he had to get out there and be the one."

* * *

IN OCTOBER 1974, Harrison arrived in Los Angeles to begin rehearsals and to finish his own album, *Dark Horse,* begun a year ago in London. He chose to squeeze both projects–plus a single, also called "Dark Horse"–into a three-week period. He promptly lost his voice and, at a press conference on the eve of the tour, announced as much, and joked that he might very well go out the first few shows and do instrumentals.

That might not have been a bad idea. Harrison did in fact start each show without singing, presenting himself as just one of nine band members, playing a well-arranged, tension-and-release number called "Hari Good Bye Express." Regarding Harrison's hoarseness, Preston later said, "He feels a little bad about it, but there's nothin' he can do, he's been working so hard."

Through Seattle, San Francisco, Oakland, Long Beach and Los Angeles, Harrison sounded the same, and so did the reviews. In San Francisco, Phil Elwood of the *Examiner:* "Never a strong singer, but a moving one, Harrison found that he had virtually no voice left and had to croak his way through even the delicate 'Something.'" In Los Angeles, Robert Kemnitz of the *Herald:* "Opening with 'While My Guitar Gently Weeps,' the band was cooking so fast and hard that Harrison's vocal shortcomings were easily overlooked. But as he tore into 'Something,' shouting the lyrics of a most tender ballad like a possessed Bob Dylan on an off night, you realized the voice was almost gone."

In Los Angeles, during the first of three shows at the Forum, Harrison told the house, "I don't know how it feels down there, but from up here, you seem pretty dead." Later, his voice breaking, he lectured someone in the audience who'd screamed out a request for "Bangla-Desh": "I have to rewrite the song. But don't just shout 'Bangla-Desh.' Give them something to help. You can chant 'Krishna, Krishna, Krishna,' and maybe you'll feel better. But if you just shout 'Bangla-Desh, Bangla-Desh, Bangla-Desh,' it's not going to help anybody."

Finally, after he'd cooled down a bit, Harrison apologized for the way things seemed to be going.

The next day, Harrison played two shows at the Forum with less-than-packed houses. Most of the people who'd forked over $9.50 to see Beatle George expected a Beatle show, a rubber-soul revue, a long and winding mem-

Previous page: "The biggest obstacle in doing this show has been people's preconceptions," Harrison said of the tour. "I just would like to be George Harrison, that's all." Opposite: Preston provided some of the tour's best moments.

ory lane. Even if they'd kept up with Harrison these past few years and knew better, they still wanted a Beatle.

Harrison, from the outset, refused. At rehearsals, during the first run-through, it took two hours and eighteen songs before Harrison would do a Beatles tune–"In My Life" from *Rubber Soul*. The way horn player Tom Scott told it, Shankar had to go to Harrison to urge him to consider audience expectations "and give the people a couple of old songs; it's okay."

"George says people expect him to be exactly what he was ten years ago," said Shankar. "He's matured so much in so many ways. That's the problem with all the artists, I suppose, Frank Sinatra or anyone popular for many years. People like to hear the old nostalgia."

> *"He could have hid under the warm Beatles blanket," said the '74 tour's promoter, Bill Graham. "But he doesn't want to be a Beatle."*

"George didn't want to do 'Something' at all," said Preston, describing the rehearsals. "I knew he was gonna have to do it, and he started rebelling against it by doing it a different way, rewriting the lyrics. But at least he's doing the song." (At one show on the tour, Harrison changed the lyrics to "Something," singing, "You're asking me will my love grow/I hope so, I don't know.")

On paper, the concert sounds pretty dreadful. But it wasn't quite that bad.

For one thing, before each show there was a mood of expectation, and in Vancouver, that itself was a show. The audience ignited matches, of course, plus $1.39 butane lighters, paper torches and sparklers (which several people cleverly heaved into other parts of the crowd, hot-wiring unsuspecting victims).

Everywhere, one could still detect faint traces of

Beatlemania. A twenty-year-old woman outside the Seattle Center Coliseum spotted Harrison arriving and ran into a crowd screeching, "I saw him! I saw his glasses! I saw his nose!" A younger woman, in a George Harrison T-shirt, cried uncontrollably in the front row in Vancouver. And at the Oakland Coliseum, a crowd of four or five dozen fans stormed past a puny link of three security guards and rushed up to the stage during "Give Me Love."

Also, there was the appealing sincerity of George Harrison himself, blissed-out and beaming while committing all manner of ghastly, anti-show-business mistakes—overintroducing Shankar or Preston, imploring the audience to "have a little patience" for the Indian music before they've even heard any, constantly apologizing for his defective throat and greeting Shankar Indian-style, with a *pranam,* kneeling and touching Shankar's feet, placing his hands on Shankar's head, thus showing humility in front of his friend and teacher.

*   *   *

AT HIS PRESS CONFERENCE, Harrison explained why he did so few interviews: "I'm a musician, I'm not a talker." But now he wanted to talk. We waited through his visit with Dylan and watched Harrison's father and brother mingling with the musicians in a room decorated with Indian fabric on the walls.

Finally, just a half hour before Harrison had to return to the stage, we met. We talked mostly about immediate concerns and ended up thrusting and parrying about criticisms of his concerts. He was friendly, direct, strong-willed, tugging at his fingers now and then, digging into me with his blue eyes.

More than anything else, Harrison was thinking about his concerts and about the response so far. He spoke with more earnestness than the anger and impatience his words, on paper, might imply.

"It's not just by chance we all bumped into each other in Vancouver. I mean, that's how some people come and review the show, as if it was simple just to get it there. I mean, we went to great length and great pain and through a lot of years of life and experience to be able to be grateful to even meet each other, let alone form it into a band and then put it on the road.

"There's a lot more to it than just walking in and shouting if you're drunk or—you know, the people have

to *think* a little bit more. The audience has to sacrifice a little bit of something. They have to give a little bit of energy. They have to listen and look, and then they'll get it, they'll get something good. They think it's going to be this or that, then that itself is the barrier which stops them enjoying, and if you can just open your mind and heart, there's such joy in the world to be had."

At every concert, he said, something good had gotten across to the audience: "There's been bad moments in each show, but, I mean, it doesn't matter, because of the spirit of everybody dancing and digging it. And if you get fifty drunkards who are shouting, bad-mouthing Ravi or whatever, and you get seventeen thousand people who go out of there relatively pleased, some of them ecstatic, and some of them who happen to get more from it than they ever thought. . .

"Because I'm taping the audience every night and asking them about it, and I know we get ten people who say the show sucks, and we get a hundred who, when you say, 'Did you get what you wanted?' say, 'We got much more than we ever hoped for.' "

He had no control over his rehearsal and recording schedule, he said. "I don't have control over anything. I believe in God, and he is the supreme controller even down to the rehearsal." So his voice on "Dark Horse" is husky, "and it's more like I am right at this minute. I'm talking about the emphasis that gets put on a thing. People expect so much. If you don't expect anything, life is just one big bonus, but when you expect anything, then you can be let down. I don't let anybody down."

What about those who scrounged up $9.50 wanting at least a taste of Beatle George? Harrison leaned forward: "Well, why do they want to see if there is a Beatle George? I don't say I'm Beatle George."

"Well, one of the things you don't control . . . "

"I do control . . . "

" . . . is how the audience feels about you. The conceptions . . . "

"Okay, but I certainly am going to control my own concept of me. Gandhi says, 'Create and preserve the image of your choice.' The image of my choice is not Beatle George. If they want to do that they can go and see Wings, then . . . Why live in the past? Be here now, and now, whether you like me or not, this is what I am." ✤

By Charles M. Young

RS 229 ❖ DECEMBER 30, 1976

GEORGE'S

Keys to the Good Life

A new album and the old sense of humor

THE MEETING was very strange. I didn't know if Kissinger wanted to see me, or if he thought I wanted to see him," says George Harrison on the Warners jet flying from Washington to New York on the last leg of a promo blitz for his new album, *Thirty-three and 1/3.*

"Somebody suggested we go to the State Department instead of the Smithsonian aerospace place, and I got this message saying to go meet him in his office. He said he wasn't seeing many people these days because he was moving out soon. I told him I was on a promotional tour. He asked, 'What are you promoting?' I said, 'Me.' Then he mentioned he had met another one of the Beatles but wasn't sure which. He thought it was the one with a Japanese wife. 'Oh, you probably mean John,' I said. 'He was having trouble with Immigration.' He asked if I was having trouble with Immigration and I said, 'No, I still live in England.' I gave him a T-shirt and a copy of *Autobiography of a Yogi,* and he said goodbye."

It was a flash of the old absurdist humor, reminiscent of that wonderful culture clash when Harrison con-

fronted the youth marketing man in *A Hard Day's Night,* and reassuring because the former Beatle has fallen so deeply into legal and personal troubles over the past few years—among them a plagiarism suit, an album delayed by a threatened A&M Records lawsuit, postponed tour plans and a missed appearance on *Saturday Night Live* with old friend Eric Idle—that you wonder if he genuinely finds anything funny, or if his guru just told him that jokes could ease the pain.

"It almost got me depressed, but then I thought, 'Sod it,'" he says of the plagiarism suit recently decided against him, with the money settlement still to be worked out. The case is likely to set new legal precedents, the judge having ruled that Harrison unconsciously stole the melody of "He's So Fine" for "My Sweet Lord" on his first solo album. "People know these suits are just aggravation. They know you hate to spend time in court and will do anything to get out."

Harrison's response to the suit is best stated in "This Song," an upbeat single with a pun on Bright Tunes Publishing, which won the suit. "This tune has nothing Bright about it/This tune ain't good or bad and come ever what may/My expert tells me it's okay."

* * *

IT'S SIXTY-TWO WITH A BULLET," he says with a touch of worldly pride incongruous in a man who is to fly to India in a couple of days to attend the birthday celebration of his friend Sai Baba. Dressed in blue jeans and an expensive sweater, Harrison almost literally glows with good health. He was stricken with hepatitis just a few months ago but now appears better than he has in years. Even his teeth, which once rivaled Keith Richard's for legendary rottenness, are solid and white.

To the obligatory reunion question, he responds, "The Beatles were other people a long time ago. They're for the history books, like the year 1492. It was cute the way the ad in the *Times* tried to put the responsibility for saving the world on our shoulders."

The subject changes to religion, particularly, the thousands of glassy-eyed fanatics who wander the streets of New York in search of converts. I paraphrase a quote from the Danish theologian Sören Kierkegaard: "There are many people who reach their conclusions about life like schoolboys: They

cheat their master by copying the answer out of a book without having worked out the sum for themselves." Guru followers, I suggest, haven't worked out the sum for themselves.

"I know your attitude," he responds. "I almost became a Catholic when I was eleven or twelve, but I couldn't relate to Christ being the only son of God—he was it and there was nothing more. The only things that really made an impression were the oil paintings and statues of the cross. Later, on a tour of Australia, our press officer, Derek Taylor, said in *Time* or somewhere, 'I'm anti-Christ, but *they're* so anti-Christ it frightens me.' Well, I wasn't anti-Christ. I was anti-bullshit. You've got to experience the answers for yourself. A good book or guru can tell you how to experience them."

The new album is his best work in a long time, with several strong songs, particularly on side one. The general attitude is definitely "It almost got me depressed but sod it." His main themes are madness in the material world and two types of love: religious and romantic, a distinction he doesn't always make clear. You can't tell if he is singing to God or to a woman.

"I've heard that said before. I think all love is part of a universal love," he says. "When you love a woman, it's the God in her that you see. The only complete is for God. The goal is to love everyone equally, but it doesn't necessarily work out that way."

One of Harrison's unequally large loves is for Eric Idle. Idle, the once and future member of Monty Python, directed promotional films of Harrison singing his new "True Love" and "Crackerbox Palace."

Harrison directed a third movie of "This Song," a demented courtroom satire that is by far the best of the lot. "I'm glad to hear it," he says with more relief than pride. "It would have been awful if 'This Song' hadn't measured up to what Eric had done. I have a real future in film clips."

* * *

WHILE VISITING NEW YORK, Harrison appeared on *Saturday Night Live.* During the taping, Harrison asks the studio audience if they have any questions. Hearing none, he provides one himself: "Is it true John Denver is splitting up?"—a reference to the Random Notes parody in Eric Idle's *The Rutland Dirty*

Weekend Book. Suddenly he breaks into a rousing rendition of "Rock Island Line" with his guitar that has the audience clapping along and Paul Simon joining in on the chorus. Simon answers a little later with "The Boxer." During the actual taping, the pair sing charming versions of "Here Comes the Sun" and "Homeward Bound." The harmonies are just about perfect. When Harrison sings one verse alone on "Homeward Bound" with his quavering voice both evocative and controlled, the effect is stunning.

Previous page: The reclusive Harrison comes out of hiding. Above: Celebrating the release of 'Thirty-three and 1/3' at Friar Park. "The Beatles are for the history books," he said. "Like the year 1492."

I sit with Olivia Arias, a former employee of Dark Horse and Harrison's girlfriend of two years. "I don't think we should use the words *follower* or *devotee* to describe me," she says of her contact with Guru Maharaj Ji. " . . . I practice the meditation techniques he has revealed and I'm grateful."

Arias shares Harrison's bony beauty and preoccupation with God. Both are strict vegetarians. If there is an ounce of fat on either, it is well hidden. "We have a nice relationship," she says. "When you strive for something higher in the next world, you have a much easier time in this one." I ask the secret of their good health. "We both take acupuncture and herbs," she answers. "I was with him when he got sick in England. I said, 'Hey, you're turning yellow,' but he wouldn't believe me. The regular doctor just said to stay in bed. Our Los Angeles doctor sent herbs that we boiled and ate every morning. It really worked."

Caryl Starling of *The Muppets* walks over and presents Arias with a stuffed replica of Kermit the Frog. "Look, he's doing one of our meditation techniques," Arias says, sitting Kermit in the lotus position and placing his hands over his eyes. "He's blissed-out." ✳

By Anthony DeCurtis

RS 511 ∗ OCTOBER 22, 1987

1987

GEORGE HARRISON

Gets Back

He invites a reporter for a rare visit to Friar Park

Y OU LOOK LIKE the only person here who might be from New York," is the first thing George Harrison says when he picks me up at the train station in Henley-on-Thames, the London suburb where he lives with his wife, Olivia, and their son, Dhani. I was told that someone would meet me and drive me to Harrison's estate, called Friar Park, but I didn't expect the man himself. Harrison is smiling and friendly as he leads me to a black Ferrari 275 GTB for the short drive to his home.

George Harrison has spent most of his time since the Beatles' split-up avoiding the public eye. "Got out of the line of fire," is how he puts it on one of the songs on his new album, *Cloud Nine.*

The psychic roller coaster that the Beatles rode in both their public and private lives was a large part of the reason for Harrison's withdrawal. The first impact of that experience for him was a disorienting sense of being swept along by something much larger than himself. "We were just kids, getting carried away on the whole snowball effect," he says. "It was later, when all that smoking reefer and LSD came about, that you started getting into thinking, actually saw what was happening. Before that, we didn't have time to think. We were just going from one gig to another and into the studio and TV studios and concerts."

134

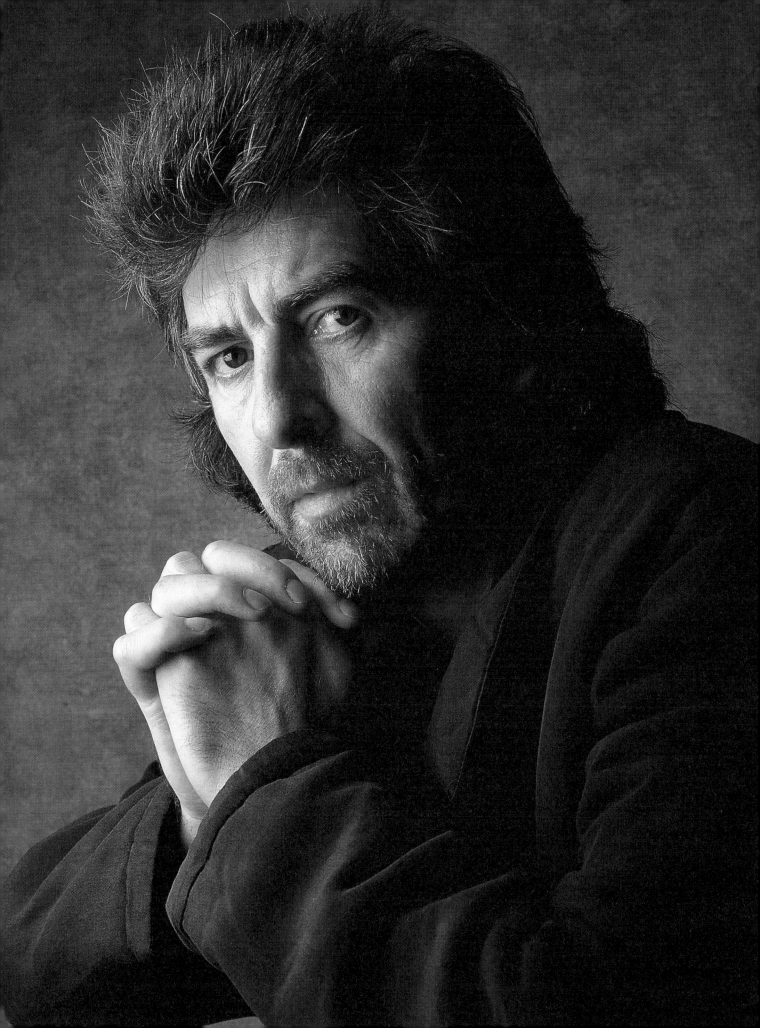

Partly as a result of their outspokenness about their experiences with "reefer and LSD"–and John Lennon's famous remark about the Beatles being "more popular than Jesus Christ"–the Beatles began distancing themselves from the less open-minded segment of their audience. They paid a price for their freedom. "We were loved for one period of time, then hated," Harrison says. "We went from being the cute, lovable moptops to these horrible, bearded hippies–and back out of it again. The press put so much praise on you that the only thing left to do is start knocking you down."

Throughout all the external shifts, Harrison, the youngest member of the group, stood in the shadow of Lennon and Paul McCartney as a songwriter and had a difficult time both establishing himself within the group and defining his own identity once the band broke up. Harrison's interests in Eastern music and mysticism helped center him, but they also contributed to his image as a stern figure outside the pop-culture mainstream. To free himself from his past, Harrison often went far out of his way to deny the significance of the Beatles and to discourage any expectations of himself as a former member of the most popular band in history.

Over time, however, he has grown much more relaxed about the events that took place all those years ago, and he has become more outgoing as a result. Last June he appeared at the Prince's Trust benefit concert in London with Ringo Starr and a pickup band of musician friends, including Eric Clapton, and played two Beatles songs. He also popped up one night last spring at the Palomino club in Los Angeles and jammed with John Fogerty and Harrison's old friend Bob Dylan.

Friar Park, where Harrison spends much of his time out of the spotlight, is an apt symbol of his essentially private nature. The grounds are dominated by an enormous, ornate mansion, built by the nineteenth-century British eccentric Sir Francis Crisp, that served as a convent before Harrison bought it in 1969. "It's like Disneyland–'Give me some coupons and I'll show you this,'" he says of the tendency of visitors to be intrigued and distracted by the estate's fairy-tale-like environment. In its whimsicality, spiritual heritage and atmosphere of seclusion, Friar Park is so much the perfect home for Harrison that he has twice celebrated the place in song: in "Ballad of Sir Frankie Crisp," on *All Things Must*

Pass, and "Crackerbox Palace," on *Thirty-three and 1/3.* Friar Park also affords plenty of opportunities for one of Harrison's favorite solitary activities: the decidedly un-rock-star-ish pastime of gardening.

* * *

WHILE HARRISON HAS SHIED AWAY from the limelight through much of his post-Beatles life, he has hardly been inactive. In 1971, at the request of his friend the sitarist Ravi Shankar, Harrison organized the benefit concert for Bangladesh–a forerunner of the Band Aid and Live Aid events–that brought together many of the rock superstars of the time for the cause of famine relief. He toured America in 1974, albeit somewhat haphazardly and to mixed reviews, with a full band of his own and a virtual orchestra of Indian musicians. He wrote an autobiography, *I Me Mine,* and launched the movie company HandMade Films, which has become a highly respected force in the British film industry. He also started his own record label, Dark Horse, in 1974, produced and played on records by other artists, and maintained a consistent flow of solo albums and singles, cracking the Top Forty eleven times.

But with the failure of his last solo LP, 1982's half-hearted *Gone Troppo*–which drew part of its inspiration from his fondness for tropical climes–Harrison seemed to grow disillusioned with the music industry. "I just think he wasn't interested, personally," says keyboardist Gary Wright, who is Harrison's longtime friend and who cowrote the pop-y "That's What It Takes" for *Cloud Nine.* "Sometimes when you make a record and it's not successful, you just don't want to go through that process for a while. You want to have your wounds heal." At Friar Park, Harrison reflected on his self-imposed retreat from the music business and said, "I got a bit tired of it, to tell you the truth. It's one thing, making a record, but if nobody plays it on the radio, what's the point of spending months in the studio?"

In addition, Harrison was less than wildly enthusiastic about the direction of popular music in the Eighties. "On the album before *Troppo,* which was *Somewhere in England,*" Harrison says, "I wrote this song called 'Blood From a Clone': 'They say they like it/But now in the market/It may not go well/Because it's too laid-back/It needs some oom-pah-pah/Nothing like Frank Zappa/And not New Wave/They don't play that crap/Try beating your head on a brick wall/Hard like a stone/Don't have time for the music/They want the blood from a clone.' That kind of thing got me a bit pissed off. It was good to get that off my chest, but by the time I'd not made a record for a few years, I was relaxed and cool about everything."

While cooling, Harrison continued to write songs and record at his twenty-four-track home studio and occasionally jammed with guitarist friends who live nearby, including Dave Gilmour of Pink Floyd, Bad Company axeman Mick Ralphs and Alvin Lee, formerly of Ten Years After. When in 1985 he began to feel that he might want to make a new album, he started thinking about possible producers. Though Harrison had never met him, Jeff Lynne–the leader of the Seventies symphonic-pop band Electric Light Orchestra–immediately came to mind. That Lynne's work with ELO always revealed a strong Beatles influence couldn't have escaped Harrison's notice, but Harrison emphasizes other factors.

"He's a guitarist, he's a songwriter, he's had his success," Harrison says of Lynne. "Just from the records, I thought he would be good, if we got on together. It was really a question of finding somebody to get in touch with him without saying, 'Well, look, right down the line from now I'm going to try to make a record, and you're it'–and frighten the fellow away. But that *was* in the back of my mind."

Lynne, of course, was smart enough not to take the ex-Beatle's invitation–passed along through guitarist and producer Dave Edmunds, a mutual friend–at all lightly. "I was in Los Angeles, actually, at the time," Lynne says. "Dave Edmunds said to me, just matter-of-fact, 'Oh, by the way, I forgot to tell you, George Harrison would like you to produce some stuff with him.' You know, 'by the way.' If I could've picked one guy I wanted to work with, it would have been George. I was stunned, really."

While Lynne had broken ground both with the cult-favorite band the Move in the Sixties and later with ELO, he was walking down a path trod by some formidable people when he agreed to work with Harrison. Not only had Harrison made some of the greatest records in pop-music history with the Beatles and their producer, George Martin, but *All Things Must Pass*– which included such classic Harrison tracks as "My Sweet Lord," "Beware of Darkness," "Isn't It a Pity" and "What Is Life"–was coproduced by none other than Phil Spector. Spector had first worked with the Beatles on John Lennon's "Instant Karma" and on the group's *Let It Be,* and he also oversaw the production of the live album from the Concert for Bangladesh. Fortunately for Lynne, Harrison is not awed by his own past.

About the creative breakthrough that *All Things Must Pass* seemed to represent, Harrison says simply, "Don't forget, John and Paul had been more satisfied from their ego point of view, having written all those tunes with the Beatles. Especially after 1966, I was starting to write loads of tunes, and one or two songs per album wasn't sufficient for me.

"By the time *All Things Must Pass* came, it was like being constipated for years, then finally you were allowed to go," he says, laughing. "I had seventeen tracks, and I didn't really want to chuck any away at the time–although I'm sure lots of them in retrospect *could* have been chucked away. I wanted to get shut of them so I could catch up to myself."

As for working with Spector, who is nearly as well known for his excesses as for his studio prowess, Harrison says, "He's been a bit outrageous, but he was very sweet. He was like a giant person inside this frail little body. I had a lot of laughs with Phil and a lot of good times. But I had a lot of bad times, as well. Most of the stuff I did with Phil, I ended up doing about 80 percent of the work myself. The rest of the time I was trying to get him into hospital or out of hospital. He'd be breaking his arm and, you know"–he shoots a knowing glance–"various other things."

Harrison and Lynne's working arrangement for *Cloud Nine* was a good deal more straightforward. They met for two weeks in early January at the Friar Park studio and laid down the basic rhythm tracks for about seventeen songs. Reconvening at regular intervals through late summer, they gradually narrowed their focus until they were left with the eleven songs that ended up on the album. Along the way they were joined in the sessions by Eric Clapton, drummers Ringo Starr, Jim Keltner and Ray Cooper, keyboardists Elton John and Gary Wright, and sax man Jim Horn.

Despite the shifting cast of characters, collaborating with Lynne gave Harrison the enjoyable feeling of being

in a band again. "The Beatles were a little unit on their own," he says. "We grew up together, we played all our apprenticeship together in Liverpool and Germany. We completely understood each other. Having Jeff Lynne, for me it was like, 'Now I'm back in a group.' We share responsibilities, we share ideas." Having Starr on hand also helped Harrison feel comfortable. "Ringo is like myself with the guitar," Harrison says. "I don't play it that often, I don't practice. Ringo may not play the drums from one year to the next, but when he picks up his sticks and gets his drum skins tightened right, he'll just *rock* and play just like he played in the old days."

Page 135: Harrison at age forty-four: "I wouldn't say I'm absolutely God-conscious. But, basically, we all want love." Above: At Friar Park in '87.

Harrison and Lynne were in complete agreement about what the songs on *Cloud Nine* should sound like on record. "I think he feels the same as me," Lynne says of Harrison's sense of sonic proportion amid the high-tech electronic din of so many Eighties records. "He didn't want all this banging and clattering going on."

Lynne defined a crisp, bright, neatly textured sound

that sidesteps trends and still manages to set Harrison squarely in the Eighties. "George is the king of rock & roll slide guitar," Lynne says with glee, and Harrison's sinuous, gently weeping leads are prominently featured on the album, especially on the title track, where he duels exquisitely with his longtime buddy Clapton. The ballads "Just for Today," "Someplace Else" and "Breath Away From Heaven" subtly capture the mood of prayerful, detached contemplation that is still at the center of Harrison's spiritual life. The album's first single, "Got My Mind Set on You," which was written by Rudy Clark and recorded by R&B singer James Ray, is the sort of cocky early-rock kicker that formed Harrison's musical tastes and that he still listens to regularly. And "This Is Love," "That's What It Takes" and "Fish on the Sand" find Harrison mining the pop vein that yielded many of his catchiest songs of the Seventies.

The jaunty "Wreck of the Hesperus"–with its hearty assertion, "I'm not the wreck of the Hesperus/Feel more like the wall of China. . . . I can rock as good as Gibraltar"–challenges the dimensional image of Harrison as the blissed-out moptop in the sun, dotingly gardening behind the wall of Friar Park. "I don't know if people actually think along the lines of 'Well, he's getting old,' " says Harrison, who looks composed and distinguished, if somewhat weathered, at forty-four. "But I've thought that people must be thinking that. It's really a funny song. When I started writing it, I just opened my mouth and those first two lines came out. I thought, 'Oh, okay,' and continued along that theme"–he hesitates and laughs–"until you get to the middle eight, and I suddenly go into a vicious attack on the press!"

The blasts at "poison penmen" and "brainless writers" in "Wreck of the Hesperus" are echoed in the media bashing of "Devil's Radio," with its assault on gossip journalism. Harrison still smarts from the intensity of the media gaze fixed on the Beatles and, in the Seventies, on his own private life, thanks to the love affair between Harrison's first wife, Pattie Boyd, and his close friend Eric Clapton.

"I've observed it, I've been a subject of it to a degree, I may still be that," he says about media gossip of the sort delineated in "Devil's Radio." "The song came about because I passed a church in a little country town in England that had a billboard outside it saying, GOSSIP–THE DEVILS' RADIO. DON'T BE A BROADCASTER. I've always kept away from that–though I've done my share–because with my past I've tended to be one of the people being gossiped about. It's such a waste of time."

The delightful Sixties goof "When We Was Fab"–Harrison routinely refers to the Beatles as "the Fabs"–was conceived even before Harrison and Lynne went into the studio to start working on *Cloud Nine*. Harrison and Lynne were vacationing in Australia–earning the song its working title of "Ozzy Fab"–where Harrison, who is an auto-racing aficionado, wanted to catch the Adelaide Grand Prix. "I had this guitar that somebody had loaned me," he says, "and, I don't know why, I thought I'd like to write a song like that period. And I could hear Ringo in my head, going, *One, two . . . da-ka-thump, da-ka-thump.*"

When Harrison and Lynne returned to England, they continued adding bits to the song, until it resembled the loonily textured "I Am the Walrus" more than any other Beatles track. Starr contributed his patented drum sound–"Those little fills are just pure Ringo," Harrison says–and Harrison even played sitar at the song's close. "It's got complete joke words," Harrison

says about the song's lyrics, which include such parodic gems as "Caresses fleeced you in the morning light." But there's enough nostalgic affection in the trippy grooves of "When We Was Fab" to tickle the brain cells and bring a smile to the face of any Sixties survivor.

A somewhat less benign exploitation of the Beatles' legacy was the recent Nike commercial in which Lennon's ambivalent Sixties anthem "Revolution" turned up for the soundtrack for an ad campaign announcing a "revolution in footwear." Through Apple Records, the Beatles have filed suit against Capitol/EMI Records for licensing the Beatles' original master of the song to Nike for the ad, despite Capitol's assertion that Yoko Ono insisted that Nike use the Beatles' original version.

"In a nutshell, there are all these people who have the rights to everything," Harrison says, alluding to the ownership of the Beatles' catalogue of songs by Michael Jackson and of the Beatles' recordings by Capitol Records. "The fact that the original master is used–I think we ought to have some say in that, seeing as it was our lives. The complication comes from the fact that Yoko, when she heard that they wanted it, insisted that it be the Beatles' version. The further complication is that Yoko is now–as John's estate–in effect a quarter of the Beatles or Apple.

"The history of the Beatles was that we tried to be tasteful with our records and with ourselves. We could have millions of extra dollars doing all that in the past, but we thought it would belittle our image or our songs. But as the man [Bob Dylan] said, 'Money doesn't talk, it swears.' Some people seem to do anything for money. They don't have any moral feelings at all."

* * *

IN OR OUT OF THE PUBLIC EYE, one aspect of Harrison's life that has remained consistent for more than two decades is his interest in spiritual matters. A firm believer in reincarnation, Harrison led the Beatles to Maharishi Mahesh Yogi and Transcendental Meditation in the late Sixties, and his fascination with Eastern religion and music encouraged the cross-fertilization of cultures that was such a rich aspect of that time. Yet Harrison's immersion in mystical thought also transformed his initial tag as the "quiet" Beatle to the "serious" one–mistrustful of fun, self-righteous about his beliefs, intolerant of people who didn't share his otherworldly vision

and coolly detached from problems he saw as manifestations of the "material world."

And while he's less strident now, he can still occasionally come off as removed. After a discussion one afternoon at Friar Park about how hard-hit British inner cities have been in the Thatcher years– "It's terrible, it's just like hell," he said of Brixton, a run-down section of London that was the site of street riots in the late Seventies–he suddenly pulled back into much less compassionate postures. "But I don't know, I don't know the answers," he said. "I think in the end, everybody has to go inside themselves and get spiritual. The more indi-

With fellow Travel-ing Wilbury Jeff Lynne, who pro-duced 'Cloud Nine' and the "new" Bea-tles' singles "Free as a Bird" and "Real Love" in 1995

viduals there are with inner strength, then that will manifest itself in the external world."

Harrison may no longer give his songs titles like "It Is 'He' (Jai Sri Krishna)," but understanding the depth of his spiritual convictions is essential to understanding both the man and his music. "It's still very much there," he says of his religious consciousness. "When I was younger, with the aftereffects of the LSD that opened something up inside me in 1966, a flood of other thoughts came into my head, which led me to the yogis. At that time it was very much my desire to find out. It still is, though I have found out a lot. I've gone through the period of questioning and being answered, and I feel I've got to the point where there isn't anything really that I need to know.

"Maybe in my youth, I was more exuberant about it. Now I've had more experience of it, and it's inside of me. I don't talk about it that much."

Having a child–his son, Dhani, is nine–has also gone a long way toward settling Harrison down. "I think the first thing is I stopped being as crazy as I used to be," he says, laughing, about Dhani's effect on his life, "because I want this child to have a father for a bit longer. Also, I think with a child around I can realize what it was like to be my father. At the same time, you can relive certain aspects of being a child. You can watch them and have all these flashbacks of when you were the kid. It somehow completes this generation thing."

Of course, in broader terms, "this generation thing" has been all the rage this year–with the crowd that came of age talkin' 'bout its g-g-generation yakking again and seeming as if it were never going to shut up. Powered by the release of the Beatles CDs and the twentieth anniversary of *Sgt. Pepper's Lonely Hearts Club Band* and the Summer of Love, Sixties bands dominate the media with a force they haven't shown since . . . well, the Sixties. Does Harrison think that much genuine understanding emerged from all the backward glancing?

"I think primarily it's nostalgia," he says. "Everybody can remember where they were when the Beatles sang 'I Want to Hold Your Hand' on *The Ed Sullivan Show*, or I remember where I was when President Kennedy got assassinated. It's all part of our history or our nostalgia.

"As to how much it means now," he adds, "I think that for a lot of the young kids, it's handy that this resurgence comes about. There's a lot of young kids who are starting to go back in time and listen and say, 'Hey!' Where maybe ten years ago, the Beatles were, like, nowhere to these kids, now the new generation latches onto them."

Some members of the younger generation are looking back even further than the Beatles, however. "Like, my boy's nine, and he just *loves* Chuck Berry," Harrison says. "When I did that Prince's Trust concert last June–that was the first time he ever saw me hold a guitar onstage in front of people. He's got to know a bit about the Beatles, but I've never pushed that on him or tried to say, 'Look who I used to be.' I did my two cute songs: 'Here Comes the Sun' and 'While My Guitar Gently Weeps.' He came

back after the show, and I said, 'What did you think?' He said, 'You were good, Dad, you were good [*slight pause*]. Why didn't you do "Roll Over Beethoven," "Johnny B. Goode" and "Rock & Roll Music"?' I said, 'Dhani, that's Chuck Berry's show you're talking about!' "

Dhani discovered Chuck Berry through a roundabout route. His mother, Olivia, a California girl, dug out the Beach Boys' "Surfing U.S.A." after Dhani heard the song in the movie *Teen Wolf.* Then, Harrison says, "I said, 'That's really good, but you want to hear where that came from,' and I played him 'Sweet Little Sixteen.' " It was love at first listen. "I made him a Chuck Berry tape," Harrison says, "and he takes it to school with his Walkman."

Does his father approve? "Little Richard, Chuck Berry, Jerry Lee Lewis–there hasn't been any rock & roll better than that," Harrison says plainly.

* * *

HARRISON HASN'T PUT his past entirely to rest, even as he moves confidently into the future with *Cloud Nine.* Playing the Prince's Trust concert, for example, initially presented some problems. After he was contacted about doing the show, Harrison got a call from Starr. Each had been contacted without the other knowing about it. "Ringo phoned me up," Harrison says, "saying, 'Somebody's asked me if I'm doing this Prince's Trust, and, of course, I can't really do it without playing on it with you.' I said, 'Ooo, I don't know about that.' I mean, Ringo will always be my friend, but just that made me nervous. I felt straightaway, somebody's trying to set *this* up again." *This* is the prospect of a Beatles reunion–the myth that will not be put to rest. "You know, it's one thing going on as me," Harrison says. "But if I'm going on as the Beatles, I want to be able to have some sort of control over it."

So the old paranoia may occasionally flare, but Harrison and Starr eventually did the show. The passage of time has brought its rewards. "What's happened over the years," Harrison says in conclusion, "is all these people–Eric Clapton, Bob Dylan, Ringo, whoever I come across of these old guys–we're not *old*. But you know what I mean–they're getting *better*. The older we all get–maybe it's this mellowing process or whatever–everybody seems to have gotten so much more at ease."

❉

By *Anthony DeCurtis*

RS 512 * NOVEMBER 5, 1987

1987

THE LAST

R.S Interview

Looking back on the Beatles, LSD and the Sixties

THE BEATLES *are virtually synonymous with the Sixties. Do you share the perception that that decade was special?*

I think that's a bit presumptuous. The Beatles did have a quickened and heightened experience, and maybe we packed more into those years, but I think it just happened to be the Sixties.

At what point did it become clear to you that the impact of the Beatles had become much greater than you ever could have conceived?

Well, it's all relative, because our original intention was to be in a band as opposed to having a job. The

goals were quite small, really. Then, after a few hit records in Europe, this mania thing started happening. The Americans caught on. I suppose after that it started taking on this sociological–or whatever you would call it–meaning. And then we were just as caught up in it as everyone else.

Was there a specific moment when it became clear to you that people were looking at the Beatles not only as a band but as a way of making sense of their lives?

I think it all came in small doses, because the fans of anybody–just like we were fans of Elvis and Eddie Cochran and Chuck Berry–tend to want to be like those role mod-

els. You want to have a guitar that looks like theirs or a hairstyle like theirs, or you want to be able to strut around like them. As we began having hits in England, the press were catching on to how we looked, which was changing the image of youth, I suppose. It just gathered momentum.

For me, 1966 was the time when the whole world opened up and had a greater meaning. But that was a direct result of LSD.

How did taking LSD affect you?

It was like opening the door, really, and before, you didn't even know there was a door there. It just opened up this whole other consciousness, even if it was down to, like Aldous Huxley said, the wonderful folds in his gray flannel trousers. From that smaller concept to the fact that every blade of grass and every grain of sand is just throbbing and pulsating.

Did it make you feel that your life could be very different from what it was?

Yeah, but that presented a problem as well, because then the feeling began in me of, well, it's all well and good being popular and being in demand, but, you know, it's *ridiculous,* really. I think from then on I didn't enjoy

Previous page: At home in L.A. Above: At the Concert for Bangladesh with Dylan, who showed up despite telling George, "Hey, man, this isn't my scene."

fame. That's when the novelty disappeared, around 1966, and then it became hard work.

It seems as if that time was incredibly compressed. Did you feel that sense of compression?

That year—I mean, you could say any year, really, from, say, 1965 up to the Seventies—it was, like, I can't believe we did so much, you know? But those years did seem to be a thousand years long. Time just got elongated. Sometimes I felt like I was a thousand years old.

Was it at that point that your identity as one of the Beatles began to get oppressive for you?

Yeah. Absolutely—again, with the realization that came about after the lysergic. I mean, it has a humbling power, that stuff. And the ego—to be able to deal with these people thinking you were some wonderful thing—it was difficult to come to terms with. I was feeling, you know, like *nothing.* Even now I look back and see, relative to a lot of other groups, the Beatles did have something. But it's a bit too much to accept that we're supposedly the designers of this incredible change. In many ways we were just swept along with everybody else.

Was the decision to stop touring in 1966 part of your reexamining your lives as Beatles?

Well, I wanted to stop touring after about '65, actually, because I was getting very nervous. They kept planning these ticker-tape parades through San Fran-cisco, and I was saying, "I absolutely don't want to do that." There was that movie *The Manchurian Candi-date* [about a war hero who returns home programmed for political assassination] . . . I think in history you can see that when people get too big, something like that can very easily happen. Although at the time it was prior to all this terrorism. I mean, we used to fly in and out of Beirut and all them places. You would never *dream* of going on tour now in some of the places we went. Especially with only two road managers: one guy to look after the equipment—which was three little am-plifiers, three guitars and a set of drums—and one guy who looked after us and our suits.

During that last tour, in 1966, there were also prob-lems after the band failed to attend the reception arranged for it at the presidential palace by Imelda Mar-cos [in the Philippines].

I'm very pleased to say that we never went to see those awful Marcoses, in spite of the fact that they tried to kill us. They sent people out there to beat us up. They set the whole of Manila on us. I don't know if you know the full story, but after half the people with us were beaten up, we finally got on the plane. Then they wouldn't let the plane take off. We sat there for . . . it seemed like an eter-nity. Finally they let the plane go. But they took all the money that we earned at the concerts from us.

It seems that various macabre things happened with regard to the Beatles. Obviously, later on the most tragic aspect of it would be the murder of John Lennon. But things like the "Paul is dead" rumors and the "Helter Skelter" business with Charles Manson—the Beatles were linked to the underbelly of American culture.

Exactly. I was maybe just sensing what was happen-ing or about to happen in the Sixties. We were flying into race riots in Chicago. We flew into this situation where the French and the English in Montreal were hav-ing a big fight, and Ringo was threatened. It was like, "We're going to kill him." Firecrackers would go off during the show, and we'd look around and think one of us had got it. Everywhere we went it was like that. We'd go to Japan where the students were rioting, and there'd be Beatlemania all mixed up with the politics.

Did your interest in Transcendental Meditation and other spiritual disciplines help you?

All the panic and the pressure? Yeah! Absolutely, I think. Although up until LSD, I never realized that there was anything beyond this state of consciousness. But all the pressure was such that, like the man said, "There must be some way out of here."

I think for me it was definitely LSD. The first time I took it, it just blew everything away. I had such an overwhelming feeling of well-being, that there was a God, and I could see him in every blade of grass. It was like gaining hundreds of years of experience within twelve hours. It changed me, and there was no way back to what I was before.

Did you feel relief when the Beatles broke up?

There was a certain amount of relief after that Can-dlestick Park concert. Before one of the last numbers, we set up this camera—I think it had a fisheye, a very wide-angle lens. We set it on the amplifier, and Ringo came out of the drums, and we stood with our backs to the audience and posed for a photograph, because we knew that was the last show.

Another event that seems significant from the per-spective of 1987 is the Concert for Bangladesh. It helped to inspire Live Aid and similar benefit concerts.

There were a lot of small charity shows, particularly in England. But Bangladesh was the first thing I'd ever heard of that was a big issue. Although it was many years later that Band Aid came about, it was definitely some-thing that needed doing.

Were you asked to do Live Aid?

No. I was away at the time, and I got back to England the day before the concert. When I arrived at Heathrow Airport, the press who were stationed there said to me, "Are you doing this concert, George?" I said I didn't know anything about it. I don't know where I'd been, in the South Pacific or somewhere for months.

Then I read something about it in the papers saying, "The Beatles are getting together." There were a few phone calls. I think Bob Geldof phoned my office and asked if I would like to sing "Let It Be" with Paul. But that was literally, like, the day before the concert.

And, I don't know . . . well, I was jet-lagged, for a start. I saw that they had everybody in the world in on this concert, and I didn't see that it would make that much difference if I wasn't. And also, you know, I have a problem, I must admit, when people try to get the Beatles together. They're *still* suggesting it, even though John is *dead.* They still come and say, "Why don't the Beatles get together?" Well, the Beatles can't.

One of the coups of Bangladesh was Dylan's appearance, because he had done so little since his motorcycle accident in 1966. Was he initially reluctant to do Bangladesh?

He was. He never committed himself, right up until the moment he came onstage. On the night before Bangladesh, we sat in Madison Square Garden as the people were setting up the bandstand. He looked around the place and said to me, "Hey, man, you know, this isn't my scene." I'd had so many months . . . it seemed like a long time of trying to get it all together, and my head was reeling with all the problems and nerves. I'd gotten so fed up with him not being committed, I said, "Look, it's not my scene, either. At least you've played on your own in front of a crowd before. I've never done that."

So he turned up the next morning, which looked positive. I had a list, sort of a running order, that I had glued on my guitar. When I got to the point where Bob was going to come on, I had *Bob* with a question mark. I looked over my shoulder to see if he was around, because if he wasn't, I would have to go on to do the next bit. And I looked around, and *he* was so nervous—he had his guitar on and his shades—he was sort of coming on, coming *[pumps his arms and shoulders]*. So I just said, "My old friend, Bob Dylan!" It was only at that moment that I knew for sure he was going to do it.

After the second show, he picked me up and hugged me and he said, "God! If only we'd done *three* shows."

That's incredible.

But he's fantastic, you know. There's not a lot of people in the world who I see from a historical point of view. Five hundred years from now, looking back in history, I think he will still be the man. Bob, he just takes the cake.

You've become nearly as reclusive as Dylan was back then. Your last solo tour was in 1974. Did anything happen on the 1974 tour that made playing in public seem like something you didn't want to do?

There was one thing that sticks in my mind. On one of the concerts, I think it was in Long Beach [California], instead of leaving right after the show, I waited till all the audience had gone. I was just hanging around the stadium, and I watched them bulldozing. They had a

bulldozer in the middle—you know that "festival seating" situation, where everybody's standing up—and they were bulldozing all the rubble left by the audience. There were *mountains* of empty bottles of gin and bourbon and tequila and brassieres and shoes and coats and trash. I mean, it was *unbelievable.*

Another thing—you know, that rock band I was in, they were some pretty heavy-duty people. We had been known in the past to smoke some reefer ourselves. But I'd go on out there, and you'd just get stoned, there was so much reefer going about.

What was your relationship with John during that period when he was living in New York?

I didn't often go to New York, but when I was in New York, I'd go see him, and he was nice. He was always enthusiastic. That period where he was cooking bread and stuff, I always got an overpowering feeling from him. Almost a feeling that he wanted to say much more than he could, or than he did. You could see it in his eyes. But it was difficult.

In what way?

Well, you'd read all these stories—and they'd keep coming all the time—about how the Beatles didn't mean a thing. That he was the only one who had a clue about anything—and the wife. There was a definite strained relationship right from the White Album. There was a lot of alienation between us and him. It was particularly strained because having been in a band from being kids, then suddenly we're all grown up and we've all got these other wives. That didn't exactly help. All the wives at that time really drove wedges between us. And then, after the years, when I saw John in New York, it was almost like he was crying out to tell me certain things or to renew things, relationships, but he wasn't able to, because of the situation he was in.

Did you feel the two of you might have gotten close again if he hadn't been murdered?

No, I only felt *physically* un-close to him, because we'd gone through too many things. You know, the very first time we took LSD, John and I were together. And that experience together, and a lot of other things that happened after that, both on LSD and on the meditation trip in Rishikesh—we saw beyond each other's physical bodies, you know? That's there permanently, whether he's in a physical body or not. I mean, this is the

goal anyway: to realize the spiritual side. If you can't feel the spirit of some friend who's been that close, then what chance have you got of feeling the spirit of Christ or Buddha or whoever else you may be interested in? "If your memory serves you well, we're going to meet again." I believe that.

With members of the International Society for Krishna Consciousness, 1969: "You can destroy our planet, but the souls keep going."

One final thing. What's your sense about the future? Are you hopeful? Feeling positive?

In one way I feel pessimistic. When you see the rate that the world is being demolished—people polluting the oceans and chopping down all the forests—unless some-body puts the brakes on soon, there isn't going to be any-thing left. There's just going to be more and more people with less and less resources. In that respect, I feel very sad. But at the same time, I have to be optimistic. I think that even if the whole planet blew up, you'd have to think about what happens when you die. In the end, "Life goes on within you and without you." I just have a belief that this is only one little bit, the physical world is one little bit, our planet is one little bit of the physical universe, and you can't really destroy it totally. You can destroy our planet, but the souls are going to keep on going, they'll keep on getting new bodies and going onto other plan-ets. So in the end, it doesn't really matter. ❋

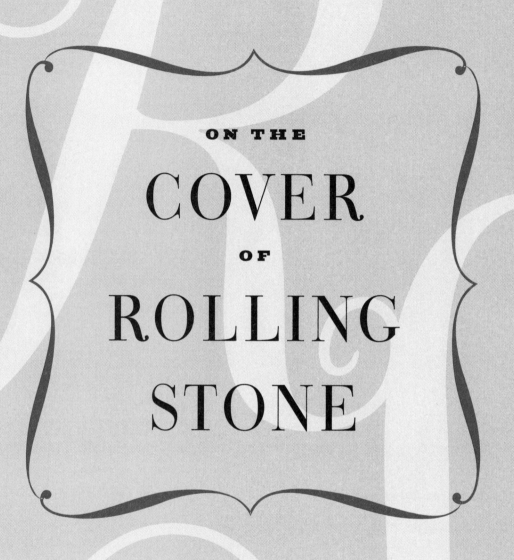

ON THE

COVER

OF

ROLLING

STONE

Harrison appeared on ROLLING STONE's cover twelve times: eight with his fellow Beatles (beginning with RS 3), three as a solo artist and once after his death. ✻

RS 3

December 14, 1967

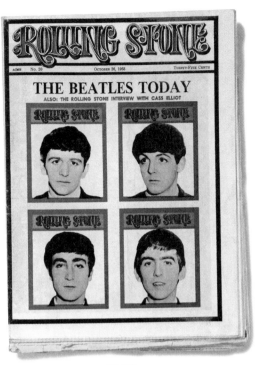

RS 20

October 26, 1968

RS 24

December 21, 1968

RS 46

November 15, 1969

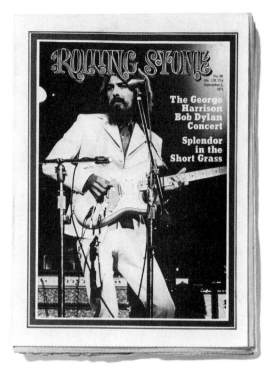

RS 90

September 2, 1971

RS 172

October 24, 1974

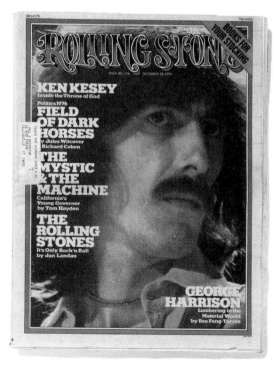

RS 176

December 19, 1974

RS 217

July 15, 1976

RS 415

February 16, 1984

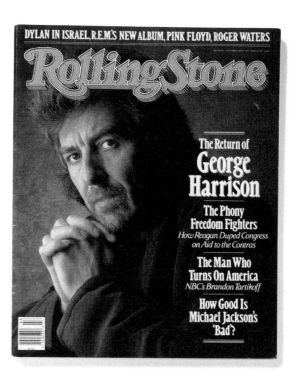

RS 511

October 22, 1987

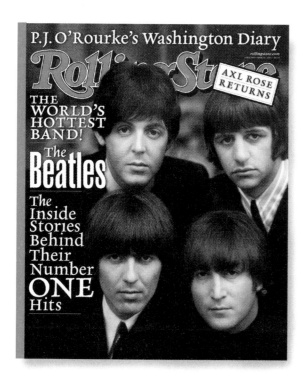

RS 863

March 1, 2001

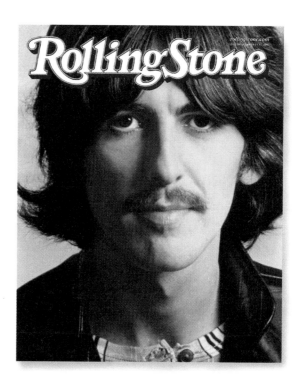

RS 887

January 17, 2002

SNAPSHOTS

FROM A

ROCK & ROLL LIFE

Thirty Years of
GEORGE IN RANDOM NOTES

Above: Harrison arrives in New York with Pattie Boyd and the master tapes. Left: With the finished album, which was released in 1970 and produced three hit singles.

SPECIAL DELIVERY:
ALL THINGS MUST PASS

{ *RS 71, November 26, 1970* }

"THERE ARE GOING to be three new Beatles albums by Christmas," Random Notes reported in November 1970. "They're all solo efforts." George Harrison's *All Things Must Pass* was the second solo release since the breakup of the Beatles (Paul McCartney's was the first), and he wasn't taking any chances with the master tapes, personally flying them to New York from London. "Among the songs," we reported, "will be Harrison's version of Dylan's 'If Not for You,' but it is doubtful that any songs from a twelve-hour session with Dylan will show up, because apparently it wasn't really all that good a session, musically, and neither Dylan nor Harrison is pleased with it." *All Things Must Pass* was a massive three-record set (priced at less than ten dollars, at Harrison's request). In 2000, as he prepared a reissue release of *All Things*, Harrison spoke to ROLLING STONE about his surplus of songs and his difficulty in getting them on Beatles albums. "It was like having diarrhea and not being able to go to the toilet," he said. "I think people were surprised to see, 'Oh, he writes songs, too.'"

IT ALMOST HAPPENED

{ *RS 95, November 11, 1971* }

ALMOST IS not enough," reported Rolling Stone. "Bob Dylan, John Lennon, George Harrison, Chuck Berry and Bo Diddley nearly jammed in New York last week." News of the surprise jam–scheduled to take place during the all-star Seventh Rock and Roll Revival–was leaked to a local radio station; after a few angry calls from Lennon, it was canceled. "On the night of the supposed jam," the story said, "the seating section reserved for the Lennon-Harrison-Dylan party was filled with various Apple employees."

MEETING THE PREZ

{ *RS 178, January 16, 1975* }

ASPECIAL GUEST SHOWED UP at George Harrison's Salt Lake City gig in 1974: Jack Ford, the twenty-two-year-old son of President Gerald Ford. "He was just crazy about the music," remembered Harrison's horn player Tom Scott. Jack phoned up his Dad, and by the time the band got to Washington, D.C., a tour of the White House had been arranged. Harrison became the first rock star to get an official greeting from a U.S. president. After some impromptu jamming on the White House piano, Harrison, Scott, Billy Preston and Ravi Shankar were ushered into the Oval Office. "George was great at breaking the ice," said Scott. "The funniest thing was when the president exchanged his WIN button for George's OM button."

"The Fords are just a regular old groovy American family," said Scott: Preston (left) and Harrison goof with the Prez.

THE CONCERT FOR BANGLADESH

{ *RS 90, September 2, 1971* }

I**T WASN'T ONLY** the glamour of the event," Randoms said of George Harrison's Concert for Bangladesh, "or the brilliance of the music or even the pantheon gathered onstage. It was a brief, incandescent revival of all that was best about the Sixties." Harrison brought along a twenty-seven-piece band (including Eric Clapton and Ringo Starr) to raise money for Pakistani refugees. Bob Dylan performed live in New York for the first time in five years. As for the after-party, Randoms said, "The booze flowed like booze. When the sun came up, Keith Moon knocked over a snare drum, stared at it, then kicked over the whole set. The night was over."

Harrison and Dylan: the highlight of the Bangladesh concert

❖ ❖ ❖

The "quiet" Beatle in a loud suit, 1974

HERE COMES THE SON

{ *RS 274, September 21, 1978* }

I**N SEPTEMBER 1978**, Random Notes reported the birth of Harrison's first and only child, a five-and-a-half-pound boy named Dhani, with his second wife, Olivia. In the summer of 2001, both parents attended Dhani's graduation from Brown University.

Harrison with Olivia and Dhani

U.S. TOUR 1974

{ *RS 179, January 30, 1975* }

H**E COULD HAVE** gone the easy way," said promoter Bill Graham in 1974. "He could have hid under the warm Beatles blanket." Instead, on his twenty-two-date tour of America, George Harrison took the hard road, trying to force Indian music (Ravi Shankar opened) and jazzy instrumentation on audiences across the country. "He lost his voice on day one," remembered Eric Clapton, "and there was a lot of dope and drink going on, which didn't help him recover." Harrison kept playing what he wanted and shrugged off the criticism. "[It] just makes me stronger," he said. "The more they try to knock me down, the more determined I am."

THE LOVE TRIANGLE

{ *RS 294, March 27, 1979* }

GEORGE HARRISON WROTE "Something" about her, and she inspired Eric Clapton's "Layla." The lucky girl was Pattie Boyd, who Harrison had met on the set of *A Hard Day's Night* in 1964 and wed two years later. The couple split in 1974 after eight years of marriage, and Boyd began dating Harrison's pal Clapton. Clapton married Boyd in 1979, with Paul McCartney, Mick Jagger, Ringo Starr and even Harrison attending the May 19 party. "It was fun at the time," Clapton said of the tryst, "like one of those movies where you see wife-swapping. [But] it devastated all three of us." Harrison, at the time, did not seem bothered. "I'd rather she be with him than some dope," he said. Still, Clapton felt awkward playing "Layla" whenever Harrison was in the crowd: "I always wondered what the hell was going through his mind."

*Harrison wrote "Something" about Boyd.
Clapton wrote "Layla" for her.*

❋ ❋ ❋

*George and Olivia, with newlyweds Ringo and Barbara,
and Paul and Linda. Barbara's son Gianni samples the icing.*

RINGO'S WEDDING DAY

{ *RS 345, June 11, 1981* }

HUNDREDS OF FANS crowded in front of London's Marylebone Registry office on April 27, craning for a glimpse of the closest thing they'd ever see to a Beatles reunion. The McCartneys and the Harrisons were on hand to celebrate Ringo Starr's wedding to Barbara Bach. The Fab Three (plus Linda) had recently united to record "All Those Years Ago," a tribute to John Lennon, which appeared on Harrison's album *Somewhere in England*. Rumors swirled about a new Beatles album; it never materialized.

Two of us: Starr and Harrison rock the royals in 1987.

PRINCE'S TRUST GALA

{ *June 6, 1987* }

WHILE IT WAS hardly the Beatles reunion predicted by the press, the highlight of the Prince's Trust Rock Gala—an annual charity event then held in the presence of Prince Charles and Lady Diana—was the rare appearance of two Beatles onstage together. At the climax of the concert, George Harrison and Ringo Starr performed with Eric Clapton and Jeff Lynne. Then, during the second night's finale, Starr led the Wembley Arena crowd through a singalong of "With a Little Help From My Friends."

✳ ✳ ✳

GEORGE HARRISON CLOSE?

{ *RS 379, September 30, 1982* }

TWENTY-THREE years after the birth of the Beatles, their hometown of Liverpool renamed four local streets in their honor. Paul McCartney Way, John Lennon Drive, George Harrison Close and Ringo Starr Drive were all designated in a housing project on the outskirts of town. None of the surviving Beatles attended the ceremony. "We just put the street signs up," a local spokesman told Random Notes at the time. "As high as we possibly could. Because souvenir hunters *acquire* them, shall we say. Penny Lane has not had a sign for nearly six months."

BABY, CAN I DRIVE YOUR CAR?

{ *RS 395, May 12, 1983* }

AS RACING BUFF George Harrison watched from the pits, a host of hot-footed celebrities put their pedals to the metal at the Toyota Pro/Celebrity race in Long Beach, California. The winner? Ted Nugent. "Most musicians want to be athletic stars of some sort," said Harrison, who has a soft spot for fast cars. "My fantasy is to be a race-car driver."

Harrison enjoys a day at the races.

Harrison and Clapton at Tokyo's Egg Dome

LIVE IN JAPAN

{ *RS 623, February 6, 1992* }

JAPAN'S A BIT OUT OF THE WAY," said Eric Clapton before he toured with George Harrison in 1991. "[George] can go onstage and get over his stage fright without being right in the international spotlight. If he came to the U.S. and saw one bad review, he'd go straight home." Talked into returning to the stage by Clapton, Harrison agreed to perform a handful of dates in Japan, his first proper tour since his poorly received swing through America in 1974. From a financial point of view, the '92 tour was a success, selling out stadiums and earning an estimated nineteen million dollars. Sadly, though, it was Harrison's last tour.

THE TRAVELING WILBURYS

{ *RS 539, November 17, 1988* }

Lynne, Dylan and Harrison (from left), filming the "Handle With Care" video

WHAT DO YOU GET when you put George Harrison, Bob Dylan, Tom Petty, Roy Orbison and Jeff Lynne in the same room? You get the Traveling Wilburys. The story goes that in the spring of 1988, Orbison and Petty were each recording solo albums at Lynne's house when Harrison dropped by and mentioned that he needed an additional track for a European EP. Everyone decided to help out, and Harrison suggested they go over to "Bob's house." Orbison was confused: "I didn't know who 'Bob' was," he told ROLLING STONE at the time. "It turned out to be Bob Dylan." The following day, the quintet wrote "Handle With Care" and was so pleased with the results that it recorded an entire album called *Vol. 1.* Tragically, Orbison died of a heart attack only weeks after it was released. Two years later, the remaining quartet released a second album, inexplicably titled *Vol. 3,* that sold more than a million copies.

✳ ✳ ✳

FANS SAY FAREWELL

{ *November 30, 2001* }

HERE COMES THE SUN," they sang at New York's Strawberry Fields in Central Park, and sure enough, as fans gathered on the overcast November day following George Harrison's death, a ray of sun cracked through the gray clouds. In the park, across the street from the Dakota, where John Lennon lived, mourners placed flowers inside Strawberry Fields' Imagine circle, as well as photographs and inscribed green apples. One sign read, "May you and John be together forever." Musicians serenaded the crowd with Beatles covers. Across the pond, British fans flocked to Abbey Road Studios to pay their respects, covering the concrete walls with bouquets, candles and scribbled tributes. And in Harrison's birthplace of Liverpool, flags flew at half mast. Said Central Park mourner Alice Harrison (no relation), who took the train in from New Jersey to say goodbye, "George stood for peace and love and music. What else is there? I've loved George since I was thirteen years old. Still do."

Top: Messages scrawled outside Abbey Road. Bottom: Strawberry Fields.

HARRISON

Family Album

PHOTOGRAPHS FROM THE
PERSONAL COLLECTION OF
OLIVIA & DHANI HARRISON

Opposite: Olivia, George and Dhani in Barbados, 2000. This page, left: In Morcote, Switzerland, 2001. Below: Sunset on Fiji's Vanua Levu Island, 2000.

Harrison loved to photo-graph his family. Opposite: Olivia in Maui, Hawaii, in 2001. This page: Dhani in Switzerland, also in 2001. That same year, Dhani ap-peared on two of his father's recordings—the reissue of 'All Things Must Pass' and a new song called "Horse to Water."

The

STORIES

BEHIND THE

SONGS

BY DAVID FRICKE

N A 'ROLLING STONE'

interview at the end of 2000, George Harrison described his music this way: "Guitars, basic drums and analog tapes–that's the way I like it. It doesn't go with trends. My trousers don't get wider and tighter every six months. My music just stays what it is, and that's it."

Beyond that modest self-assessment lies a body of work long ripe for rediscovery. His image as the brooding, reticent Beatle belied an industriousness that flourished even while he was in the group, struggling to get more than a song or two on each Beatles LP. In November 1968, he issued the first solo album by a Beatle, *Wonderwall Music,* an ambitious film soundtrack combining Western rock and sessions recorded with traditional Indian musicians. Harrison used the Beatles' boutique label, Apple, to pursue songwriting and production adventures with a wide variety of artists, from his friend and teacher Ravi Shankar and old Liverpool mate Jackie Lomax to American soul singer Doris Troy and girl-group icon Ronnie Spector. Harrison's generosity as a sessionman, aiding friends

Previous page: Linda McCartney took this intimate portrait near the group's end. Opposite: Don't bother him: Harrison taking a break backstage in East Ham, London, in 1963.

and peers on their records, was reflected in the variety of witty pseudonyms he used in many of those appearances: L'Angelo Misterioso, Hari Georgeson, George O'Hara, P. Roducer. He was a reluctant promoter of his own albums, touring North America only once, in 1974, and giving few interviews. Nevertheless, Harrison continued to record with an attention to purity–the bedrock skill and spirit of 1950s rock & roll–that never wavered.

The following is a greatest-hits survey of Harrison's musical life as a Beatle, solo artist and collaborator, touching on a dozen vital moments in his growth and accomplishments as one of rock & roll's finest, most influential songwriters and guitarists. "I don't really get proud of things I do," Harrison told ROLLING STONE. "It's not a word I use." He'd earned the right.

CRY FOR A SHADOW
Written by George Harrison–John Lennon
Produced by Bert Kaempfert
* Recorded June 22 and 23, 1961,
Friedrich-Ebert-Halle, Hamburg, Germany
* First released by Tony Sheridan on the
Mister Twist EP in France in April 1962

COMPOSED MAINLY BY George Harrison and cut almost as an afterthought at the Beatles' first professional recording session, this rough instrumental diamond was the guitarist's official bow as a songwriter. More importantly, "Cry for a Shadow" was the first original Beatles song to be recorded in a studio and the first to appear on record–six months before the British release of "Love Me Do" in October 1962. In a handwritten bio sheet from the period, Paul McCartney declared that he and John Lennon, between them, had written "around seventy songs." But it was eighteen-year-old Harrison who got top billing the first time around.

Harrison, Lennon, McCartney and original drummer Pete Best were in their second extended residency in Hamburg, Germany, when, in May of '61, the German producer and MOR bandleader Bert Kaempfert caught the Beatles at the Top Ten club, where they were sharing the bill with British singer Tony Sheridan. Kaempfert quickly put Sheridan and the Beatles in the studio together, cutting seven songs. "They represented something new to us," the session's engineer, Karl Hinze, said

in 1996. "It was loud, loud, loud."

Kaempfert had little faith in Lennon and McCartney's songwriting abilities. In October 1961, he paired rowdy covers of "My Bonnie" and "The Saints" on a single credited to Tony Sheridan and the Beat Brothers. Ironically, Kaempfert picked the raw "Cry for a Shadow" as the only Beatles composition worth recording. Originally titled "Beatle Bop" and written by Harrison as a spoof of the British instrumental group the Shadows, the melody was basically one note, chopped up into staccato and bent into piercing whines. Driven by Lennon's pulverizing rhythm guitar (hence the cowriting credit) and punctuated by McCartney's hell-raising yells, the song captured the aggressive precision of Harrison's playing in crude bloom, halfway between his first loves–the stinging pith of rockabilly gods Carl Perkins and Scotty Moore–and the incisive twang of his later solos on "I Saw Her Standing There" and "A Hard Day's Night."

"It was obvious to me that they were enormously talented," Kaempfert said of the savage young Beatles in 1964. "But nobody–including the boys themselves–knew how to use that talent or where it would lead them." Yet Kaempfert was wise enough to bring that Harrison guitar right up front–where it belonged.

DON'T BOTHER ME
Written by George Harrison
Produced by George Martin
* Recorded September 11 and
12, 1963, EMI Studios, London
* Released by the Beatles on
With the Beatles in Britain
on November 22, 1963, and
on *Meet the Beatles* in America
on January 20, 1964

THE FIRST George Harrison song to appear on a Beatles album, "Don't Bother Me" was written in mid-August 1963 while the guitarist was holed up, sick, in a hotel in Bournemouth, England, during a week-long series of Beatles shows there. Harrison was ostensibly writing about romantic desertion and the paralysis of loss, but the haunting modal melody and direct language–"So go away/Leave me alone/Don't bother me"–spoke volumes about Harrison's mounting

*In 1965, with
Boyd, practicing
the sitar, which
he introduced to
rock & roll that
year on "Norwe-
gian Wood"*

distrust of stardom and desperate
need for privacy amid the madness
of his Beatle life. At the same time
that the world was falling at his feet,
Harrison was already writing and
singing of his unease with success
and with the band that had made it possible.

"I used to have a hang-up about telling John, Paul
and Ringo I had a song for an album," Harrison admitted in 1969, "because I felt mentally, at that time, as if I
was trying to compete. And in a way, the standard of the
songs had to be good, because [John and Paul's] were
very good. I don't want the Beatles to be recording rubbish for my sake . . . just because I wrote it."

But with its despondent words charged by a hectic
Latin-rock cadence and dramatic stop-start effect in
front of the chorus, "Don't Bother Me" was more sophisticated than Harrison, as a first-time composer and
lyricist, got credit for at the time. In fact, the Beatles took
two days and seventeen takes to get it right, practically a
lifetime in the song-a-minute sessions of the time. The
other Beatles all played additional percussion—tambourine, claves, bongos—and Harrison sealed the bleak

power of the song with a short, snarling guitar solo.

As a Beatle and late-blooming songwriter, Harrison
would never fully share in the respect and spotlight ac-
corded John Lennon and Paul McCartney. But he never
doubted himself as a contender. "Sometimes it's a matter of whoever pushes hardest gets the most tunes on the
album—it's down to personalities," Harrison said in that
'69 interview. "I believe that if I'm going to sing songs
on record, they might as well be on my own."

A HARD DAY'S NIGHT
Written by John Lennon–Paul McCartney
Produced by George Martin
* Recorded April 16, 1964, EMI Studios, London
* Released by the Beatles on *A Hard Day's
Night* in America on June 26, 1964,
and in Britain on July 20, 1964

IT'S NOT OFTEN that you get to hear the Beatles
screw up in the studio, but outtakes of this immaculate raver, the title song of the Beatles' first feature film, are a fascinating study in George Harrison's
devotion to perfection. John Lennon had just finished
writing the song the day before this session, and the

group recorded it in a breakneck three hours. In take one, included on the 1995 Beatles release *Anthology 1*, one can hear Harrison searching for structure in his solo break, hesitantly pecking at a shred of a riff on his twelve-string Rickenbacker guitar. Another take, which first surfaced on a CD bootleg in the 1980s, features Harrison literally fumbling over his strings, losing his timing and missing notes.

But by the time the Beatles wrapped up the session, and the song, at ten o'clock that night, Harrison had become the decisive instrumental voice in one of the Beatles' biggest hits and defining records. That's his Rickenbacker spraying harmonics all over Lennon's opening chord, and that's Harrison picking the clean ringing arpeggio in the fade-out. And in the middle, he sculpted one of his most memorable solos—a sterling upward run of notes played twice and capped each time with a striking circular flourish, with the church-bell chime of Harrison's guitar echoed on piano by George Martin.

"George, in the studio, would spend a lot of time working out solos—nothing was done really fast," says Beatles engineer Geoff Emerick, who worked on this session. "Everything was a little bit harder for him—nothing quite came easily." But Harrison's studiousness was a vital component in the Beatles' working methods, an important balancing factor between Lennon's impetuosity and Paul McCartney's melodic ease. "Seeing him striving in the studio with his guitar," Emerick says of Harrison, "it was clear that in his mind he was trying to further himself as a musician."

EVERYBODY'S TRYING TO BE MY BABY

Written by Carl Perkins

✳ Recorded November 25, 1964, Playhouse Theatre, London

✳ Released by the Beatles on *Live at the BBC* in 1994

O**N MAY 31**, 1964, at a Beatles postshow party in London, George Harrison walked up to one of the invited guests, visiting rockabilly guitar god Carl Perkins, and, after a quick introduction, asked Perkins point-blank: What key was "Honey Don't" in? Perkins replied that he'd written the song in the key of E. Harrison turned to John Lennon and cracked, "I told you we weren't doing it right."

In their formative and early-fame years, the Beatles covered more songs by Perkins than by any other single artist. Among the eleven songs written and/or recorded by Perkins in the Beatles' stage, studio and BBC radio songbook were "Honey Don't," "Matchbox," "Sure to Fall (In Love With You)," "Blue Suede Shoes" and "Everybody's Trying to Be My Baby," a tongue-in-cheek gallop about babe magnetism from Perkins's 1958 Sun Records LP, *Dance Album of Carl Perkins.* And there was no bigger Perkins fan among the Beatles than Harrison. As a teenage rocker, he briefly used the stage name of Carl Harrison, and Harrison's deceptively elementary guitar style—the tight trebly cluck of his rhythm work and the focused golden sting of his leads—was clearly inspired by Perkins's rich country-sunshine minimalism.

"Everybody's Trying to Be My Baby" had been a Harrison vocal showcase in the Beatles' live shows as far back as 1961, and the group recorded it several times for the BBC between 1963 and 1965. At Abbey Road on October 18, 1964, the Beatles nailed the song in one take for official release on the British LP *Beatles for Sale* (the track appeared in the U.S. on *Beatles '65*). But this November 1964 BBC version is Harrison's Perkins fixation at its finest: His boyish voice is embedded in Sun-like echo, he picks his licks with roadhouse fire (note the fierce downhill break at the end of his first solo), and the rest of the Beatles swing behind him like hillbilly cats.

The song, with Perkins's playful references to rock star ego and armies of sex-mad fillies, packed extra irony for Harrison by late 1964. When Harrison sings the opening lines—"Well they took some honey from a tree/Dressed it up and they called it me"—it's a sly, mocking commentary on the weight and absurdity of his sudden, suffocating fame. In an interview with BBC host Brian Matthew that prefaced one 1964 broadcast of the song, Harrison dryly noted that "I didn't write it, even though it is conceited." The cheerful innocence of Beatlemania was already fading.

Opposite: Beatles '65: The year of 'Help!,' Shea Stadium and 'Rubber Soul.' Following pages: Touring Germany by train in June 1966, the band made its first visit in more than three years to Hamburg, where Beatlemania began.

IF I NEEDED SOMEONE

Written by George Harrison
Produced by George Martin

✳ Recorded October 16 and 18,
1965, EMI Studios, London

✳ Released by the Beatles on *Rubber
Soul* in Britain on December 3,
1965, and on *Yesterday and
Today* in America on June 20, 1966

THIS TWANGY JEWEL was the result of a remarkable exchange of influences between the Beatles and one of their favorite new bands, the Byrds. Founding Byrds Roger McGuinn, Gene Clark and David Crosby were making demos in Los Angeles as an acoustic-folk group in 1964 when McGuinn saw Harrison playing a cherry red, electric twelve-string Rickenbacker guitar in *A Hard Day's Night.* "I took my acoustic [twelve-string] and five-string banjo down to the music store," McGuinn recalls, "and traded them in for an electric twelve-string." McGuinn's Rickenbacker became the trademark sound of the Byrds and the signature instrument of the folk-rock revolution.

The Beatles returned the admiration. John Lennon and Paul McCartney attended one of the Byrds' first British shows in early 1965, and that August, on a day off from the Beatles' '65 U.S. tour, McCartney and Harrison attended a Byrds recording session in L.A. "We were recording 'She Don't Care About Time,' " says McGuinn. "I remember George was really into the Bach thing in the middle that I did"–a stirring Rickenbacker quote from "Jesu, Joy of Man's Desiring." "George said, 'That's great. I love that.' He thought it was great the way I fit it into the song."

Two months later, Harrison paid McGuinn the ultimate compliment when the Beatles recorded "If I Needed Someone," a striking blend of cool dismissal ("Carve your number on my wall and maybe you'll get a call from me") and crystalline riffing adapted from McGuinn's lead lick in "The Bells of Rhymney," on the Byrds' debut album, *Mr. Tambourine Man.* In his autobiography, *I Me Mine,* Harrison characterized the song as a set of variations on a D chord: "If you move your finger about, you get various little melodies." But to McGuinn, he gave due thanks.

"George was very open about it," says McGuinn, who was then going by his original given name, Jim. "He sent [the record] to us in advance and said, 'This is for Jim'–because of that lick."

TAXMAN

Written by George Harrison
Produced by George Martin

✳ Recorded April 20–22, 1966,
EMI Studios, London

✳ Released by the Beatles on
Revolver in Britain on August 5,
1966, and in America on
August 8, 1966

PAUL MCCARTNEY PLAYED the searing guitar solo, and John Lennon contributed to the lyrics, without credit. But in its pithy cynicism and stark rhythmic kick, "Taxman" was strictly George Harrison's triumph, a contagious blast of garage rock, and the other Beatles knew it. Harrison's crisp slap at highway robbery by Her Majesty's Government landed the prized position on *Revolver:* side one, track one.

" 'Taxman' was when I first realized that even though we had started earning money, we were actually giving most of it away in taxes," Harrison later wrote in *I Me Mine.* "Why should this be so? Are we being punished for something we had forgotten to do?" In his opening lyric salvo–"Let me tell you how it will be/There's one for you, nineteen for me"–Harrison accused the British crown of hypocrisy on top of thievery, for giving praise and MBEs with one hand while hijacking the lion's share of the Beatles' income with the other. "The government's taking over 90 percent of all our money," Ringo Starr once complained. "We're left with one-ninth [of a] pound." The Beatles were not taking sides either: "Taxman" included Lennon and McCartney name-checking, in mocking falsetto harmony, both Harold Wilson and Edward Heath, the respective heads of the Labour and Conservative parties.

Politics aside, "Taxman" represents a crucial link between the guitar-driven clang of the Beatles' 1963-65 sound and the emerging splendor of the group's experiments in psychedelia. Musically, the song is skeleton

*My Sweet George:
In 1970, Harrison
scored the first
post-Beatles Number
One hit with
"My Sweet Lord."*

funk, Harrison's choppy fuzz-toned guitar chords moving against an R&B dance beat; the structure suggests that he'd been paying close attention to British hits of that season, like James Brown's "I Got You" and "Somebody Help Me" by the Spencer Davis Group. (Latter-day Mods the Jam later adapted the riff and rhythm of "Taxman" for their 1980 British hit, "Start!") At the same time, the ragalike flavor of Harrison's vocal melody and the extra hours he and engineer Geoff Emerick spent on guitar tone, not just on "Taxman" but on the whole of *Revolver,* foreshadow Harrison's intense plunge into Indian music, and the sitar, on later songs such as "Within You Without You" and "The Inner Light."

"We were very nitpicky about the way things sounded," says Emerick of his work with Harrison. "And he probably got a bit frustrated. He'd done the guitar things and wanted to go in another direction. 'Within You Without You' was the direction he wanted to take. The other three were taken aback by it, but George was very serious about it."

Harrison never entirely abandoned "Taxman"–it was in the set list when he toured Japan with Eric Clapton in 1991. "It's a song that goes regardless if it's the Sixties, Seventies, Eighties [or] Nineties," he cracked at the time. "There's always a taxman."

WITHIN YOU WITHOUT YOU
Written by George Harrison
Produced by George Martin
* Recorded on March 15 and 22
and April 3, 1967, EMI Studios, London
* Released by the Beatles on
Sgt. Pepper's Lonely Hearts Club Band in
Britain on June 1, 1967, and in
America on June 2, 1967

GEORGE HARRISON'S MUSICAL life changed forever at a party in Los Angeles in August 1965. The Beatles were in town to play at the Hollywood Bowl. The Byrds had come up to the Beatles' rented house in the Hollywood Hills to hang out and get high. "We were on the floor exchanging guitar licks," recalls the Byrds' Roger McGuinn. At one point, McGuinn's band mate David Crosby showed Harrison "some Ravi Shankar stuff that he'd just been into, because Dick Bock at World Pacific [the studio where the Byrds made

their first demos in 1964] had been producing Ravi Shankar."

Harrison had already been introduced to the sitar earlier in '65, during the filming of the Beatles' second movie, *Help!* "We were waiting to shoot the scene in the restaurant when the guy gets thrown in the soup," he explained in an interview, "and there were a few Indian musicians playing in the background. I remember picking up the sitar and trying to hold it, and thinking, 'This is a funny sound.' " That sound became his passion, a love intensified by Crosby's enthusiasm and which reached its finest flower on record with this 1967 contribution to *Sgt. Pepper.*

By December 1965, Harrison had introduced the sitar to Beatles fans, playing it on the *Rubber Soul* recording of John Lennon's "Norwegian Wood (This Bird Has Flown)." In June 1966, Harrison met Shankar, India's reigning master of the instrument, for the first time; that fall, at Shankar's invitation, Harrison went to India for six weeks to study under the virtuoso. "I had George practice all the correct positions of sitting and some of the basic exercises," Shankar wrote in his 1969 autobiography, *My Music, My Life.* "This was the most one could do in six weeks, considering that a disciple usually spends years learning these basics." But Harrison quickly transcended his elementary abilities on the sitar, integrating the instrument's rapturous drone and the melodic and rhythmic complexities of raga into Western song with ingenious, respectful grace.

Harrison wrote "Within You Without You" in early 1967–not in India, but in England, after dinner at the home of Klaus Voormann, a close friend of the Beatles since the Hamburg, Germany, days. "Klaus had a harmonium in his house, which I hadn't played before," Harrison remembered. "I was doodling on it, playing to amuse myself when 'Within You' started to come. The tune came first; then I got the first sentence ['We were talking–about the space between us all']." He finished the song that night when he got home.

Harrison recorded the basic track on March 15 with Indian musicians recruited from the Eastern Music Circle in London, playing tabla, *dilruba* (a sitarlike instrument), *swarmandal* (an Indian style of zither) and tamboura; Harrison and Beatles assistant Neil Aspinall played tamboura as well. (No other Beatle ap-

peared on the final track.) At a marathon session of nearly twelve hours on April 3, Harrison overdubbed his own sitar, some acoustic guitar and a haunting lead vocal; an eleven-piece string section accented the Indian instrumentation, using a score written by George Martin. The result was at once beautiful and severe, a magnetic sermon about materialism and communal responsibility in the middle of a record devoted to gentle Technicolor anarchy. Harrison's growing estrangement from the other Beatles can also be heard with piquant clarity: "We were talking–about the love that's gone so cold and the people/Who gain the world and lose their soul/They don't know–they can't see–are you one of them?"

Although "Within You Without You" was largely dismissed as an alien novelty when *Sgt. Pepper* was released in the Summer of Love, Harrison's devotion to the sound and soul of India long outlived the Beatles'

flirtations with psychedelia, later blooming all over his solo masterwork, *All Things Must Pass.* But Harrison was also enlightened enough to poke a little fun at himself. During mixdowns on April 4, he dropped in a few seconds of crowd laughter at the end of "Within You Without You," taken from a sound-effects tape in the Abbey Road library ("Volume 6: Applause and Laughter").

"I think he just wanted to relieve the tedium a bit," Martin suggested later. "George was slightly embarrassed and defensive about his work. I was always conscious of that; perhaps I didn't devote as much attention to George as I had [to Lennon and Paul McCartney]. I actually think 'Within You Without You' would have benefitted a bit by being shorter, but it was a very interesting song. I find it more interesting now than I did then."

BADGE

Written by Eric Clapton and George Harrison
Produced by Felix Pappalardi

* Recorded October 1968
* Released by Cream on *Goodbye* in March 1969

"I F HE ASKS me to do anything," Eric Clapton said of George Harrison in a 1974 ROLLING STONE interview, "he's got the best that I can give, whenever I can give it." That sentiment went both ways and was the foundation of a musical and personal friendship that lasted nearly forty years—a brotherly affection that even withstood the drama of Clapton's love for Harrison's first wife, Pattie Boyd, documented by Clapton with gripping candor on *Layla and Other Assorted Love Songs,* his 1970 album with Derek and the Dominos.

Clapton and Harrison first met in December 1964, when Clapton's band the Yardbirds landed an opening-act spot on the Beatles' Christmas-season shows at the Hammersmith Odeon in London. "The Yardbirds were on the bottom of the bill," Clapton remembered, "but all of the acts in between were sort of music-hall English rock & roll groups. And the Yardbirds were an R&B band, or even a blues band, so there was a bit of 'What's this all about?' George was checking me out, and I was checking him out to see if he was a real guitar player. And I realized he was."

Harrison, in turn, would repeatedly draw on Clapton's instrumental prowess for his own music: Clapton played the grand, aching lead guitar on Harrison's "While My Guitar Gently Weeps," on the White Album; contributed a feast of guitar to Harrison's solo debut, *All Things Must Pass;* and appeared with Harrison at the Bangladesh charity shows in New York in 1971. When Harrison returned to the road for a series of Japanese concerts in 1991, he called on Clapton to join him. "It's just an attraction we have," Harrison said during that tour, "an attraction in our lives. And it's also the way he bends the notes."

A staple of Clapton's live shows to this day, "Badge" was the pair's first official cowriting adventure, created for Clapton's last album with Cream, *Goodbye.* Harrison—listed in the original credits as L'Angelo Misterioso for contractual reasons—also played rhythm guitar on the track, and his melodic sensibility shines throughout. Although Clapton would go through two more bands—Blind Faith and the Dominos—before starting a solo career in earnest, "Badge" shows the pop influence Harrison had on Clapton as the latter began to shed his blues-purist skin.

The song is a lyrically enigmatic reflection on a love gone awry, a dark, trancelike rocker split in the middle by a marvelous bridge announced by a regal Clapton riff played through a Leslie speaker. Indeed, it was that bridge that inadvertently gave "Badge" its name. "I wrote most of the words, Eric had the bridge, and he had the first couple of chord changes," Harrison said. "I was writing the words down, and when we came to the middle bit, I wrote 'Bridge.' And from where he was sitting, opposite me, he looked and said, 'What's that—"Badge"?' So he called it 'Badge' because it made him laugh."

Memories longer than the road stretching out ahead: In the studio, 1970, during the 'Let It Be' sessions

SOMETHING

Written by George Harrison
Produced by George Martin

* Recorded February 25, April 16, May 2 and 5, July 11 and 16, and August 15, 1969, EMI Studios, London
* Released by the Beatles on *Abbey Road* in Britain on September 26, 1969, and in America on October 1, 1969

"O N FEBRUARY 25, 1969, his twenty-sixth birthday, George Harrison recorded three demos at EMI Studios in London, singing and playing guitar and piano, assisted only by engineer Ken Scott. Harrison did two takes each of "Old Brown Shoe," soon to be cut by the Beatles for a B side, and "All Things Must Pass," the title song of his 1970 solo album. He also took a single pass at a winsome ballad that he had written on piano the previous year during a break in the White Album sessions: "Something."

Harrison and the other Beatles would labor on the song for the next six months, repeatedly coming back to it during the making of *Abbey Road,* editing, arranging and rerecording it to perfection. John Lennon would later confess that "Something" was the best

song on *Abbey Road.* Released as a single in October 1969, coupled with Lennon's "Come Together," "Something" went to Number Three on *Billboard*'s Top 100 and spawned a major industry in cover versions, coming in second in the Beatles cover sweepstakes behind Paul McCartney's "Yesterday." Harrison claimed that when he wrote "Something," "in my mind, I heard Ray Charles singing it." In fact, Charles would sing it on his 1971 album, *Volcanic Action of My Soul.* And Frank Sinatra, a man with little taste or patience for rock, recorded "Something" in the 1970s, describing it as "the greatest love song of the past fifty years."

"Something" marked Harrison's commercial and artistic coming-of-age as a pop songwriter, earning him the respect he had long been denied by Lennon and McCartney—and, to some degree, by producer George Martin. "It took my breath away," Martin later said of "Something," "mainly because I never thought that

George could do it. George wrote pretty good songs by this time. He wrote some pretty rotten ones in the beginning, but he gradually developed. It was tough for him because he didn't have any springboard against which he could work, like the other two did. And so he was a loner. I first recognized that he really had a great talent when he did [*Abbey Road*'s] 'Here Comes the Sun.' But when he brought in 'Something,' it was something else. . . . It was a tremendous work—and so simple."

The song was actually two moods in one: the pillowy yearning of the verses and chorus, and the golden thunder of the bridge, the latter driven by Ringo Starr's military flourish on a high-hat cymbal, underscoring the impassioned worry in Harrison's double-tracked singing and McCartney's distinctive backing vocal. In his book *Revolution in the Head: The Beatles' Records and the Sixties,* Ian McDonald suggests that the opening lyric–"Something in the way she moves"–was "absent-mindedly taken" from James Taylor's song of the same name, which appeared on his 1968 Apple

Records debut, *James Taylor.* Harrison had attended the London sessions for Taylor's record and sang back-up vocals on another song, "Carolina in My Mind."

But the decisive time and care that went into crafting "Something" was, in the end, all Harrison's. On August 15, the final day of recording for the song, Harrison shared the conductor's podium with Martin during the string overdubs and recut his elegant guitar solo, a sparkling combination of dirty-blues-like slide and soaring romanticism. "He actually did it live with the orchestra," engineer Geoff Emerick says of that guitar break. "It was almost the same solo [as before]–note for note. The only reason I feel he wanted to redo it was emotion."

"He was always nervous about his songs," Martin said of Harrison, "because he knew that he wasn't the number one [writer] in the group. He always had to try harder than the others." But with "Something," the guitarist proved himself to his peers, and the world. "I chastised myself a little bit, that I didn't pay more attention to him in the earlier days," Martin admitted. "But then, see, when I was dealing with a couple of characters like Lennon and McCartney, who could blame me for concentrating on them? These were probably the two greatest songwriters we've ever had, and they were the ones bringing in the goods."

"George made it eventually," Martin added proudly. "He did it despite all the encouragement I should probably have given him."

IF NOT FOR YOU
Written by Bob Dylan
Produced by Bob Johnston
✳ Recorded May 1, 1970,
Columbia Studios, New York
✳ Released by Bob Dylan on
The Bootleg Series,
Volumes 1–3 (Rare and
Unreleased) 1961–1991 in 1991

"My SHARED EXPERIENCE writing a song with other songwriters is not that great," Bob Dylan said in a 1991 interview in *Song Talk.* "Of course, unless you find the right person to write with as a partner. . . . " He paused to laugh. "You're awfully lucky if you do."

Dylan didn't need anybody's help writing this rustic love song, released on his 1970 album, *New Morning,* in a version recorded a month after this session. But "If Not for You" was a cornerstone of Dylan's long creative association with George Harrison, a mutual fondness that bloomed on record and in concert through four decades. Harrison cut the song as well for his 1970 album, *All Things Must Pass,* and the pair recorded it together at a legendary session that was "a monster," according to a source quoted in a ROLLING STONE news story at the time. The evidence, finally issued twenty-one years later, did not live up to the hyperbole, but there is no mistaking the warm air of camaraderie blowing through this modest, endearing performance.

Harrison was in the audience with John Lennon when Dylan performed at the Royal Festival Hall in London in May 1965, an experience that would greatly influence the sound and language of the Beatles' next studio album, *Rubber Soul.* Dylan and the Beatles kept crossing paths over the next two years (Lennon actually appears in D.A. Pennebaker's documentary of Dylan's '66 electric tour, *Eat the Document*), but it was with Harrison that Dylan established a lasting bond. There was little preparation for this day of recording at Columbia Records' Studio B in New York: Harrison met Dylan the day before at Dylan's apartment for an informal jam. On the afternoon of May 1, the two shambled through nearly two dozen songs, a potpourri of numbers running the gamut from Dylan's own "Gates of Eden" and "Song to Woody" to the Crystals' "Da Doo Ron Ron" and Paul McCartney's "Yesterday."

The evening session was more serious: With a small combo including Charlie Daniels on bass and Russ Kunkel on drums, Dylan and Harrison worked on three songs that Dylan would rerecord in June on his own for *New Morning*–"Time Passes Slowly," "Sign on the Window" and "Went to See the Gypsy"–and another Dylan original, the eccentric "Working on a Guru." Dylan had previously attempted "If Not for You" in March at a recording date in Nashville. But at the May 1 get-together, Harrison contributed a gorgeous, pedal-steel-like guitar lick that Dylan wisely kept in the arrangement when he recut the song in June.

The excitement generated by the idea of a Dylan-Harrison collaboration was greater than the results that day. ROLLING STONE, confusing the afternoon hootenanny with the evening work, claimed "about five of the numbers are reportedly of high enough quality to merit inclusion on a future Dylan album." Britain's *New Musical Express* went even further, proclaiming DYLAN AND HARRISON WAX LP TOGETHER! In fact, nothing from that day was released at the time.

But Dylan and Harrison continued sharing songs and stages. *All Things Must Pass* featured a composition actually cowritten by Dylan and Harrison, "I'd Have You Anytime," based on a Dylan lyric that he gave to Harrison to set to music. In 1971, Dylan—who had stopped touring after his 1966 motorcycle accident—broke his sabbatical from performance to appear at Harrison's Bangladesh charity spectacular; Harrison, in turn, made a rare concert appearance in 1992 at Dylan's thirtieth-anniversary tribute concert in New York. And they did end up making not one, but two, whole albums together, in 1988 and 1990 with the Traveling Wilburys.

MY SWEET LORD
Written by George Harrison
Produced by George Harrison
and Phil Spector

* Recorded between May and August 1970
* Released by George Harrison
on *All Things Must Pass* in America
on November 27, 1970, and in
Britain on November 30, 1970

AN EIGHT-LINE PRAYER that became the first and biggest hit single of George Harrison's solo career, "My Sweet Lord" was big and bright enough in its melodic grandeur and surging profession of faith that it moved even John Lennon, a determined skeptic on the subject of religion, to reconsider his position on the divine. "I'm starting to think there must be a God," Lennon remarked admiringly of the record.

Harrison's commitment to Indian spirituality, particularly the Hare Krishna movement, was heartfelt and lifelong. He provided extensive financial assistance to the London temple founded by Swami Prabhupada and produced records by his followers for the Beatles' Apple label. In a 1984 interview, Harrison said that one of the greatest thrills of his life was seeing members of the Radha Krishna Temple performing their 1969 Harrison-produced hit, "Hare Krishna Mantra," on the British TV show *Top of the Pops.* "That was more fun re-ally than trying to make a pop hit record," Harrison said of the single. "It was the feeling of utilizing your skills to do some spiritual service for Krishna."

Harrison's triple-LP solo debut, *All Things Must Pass,* was service on a larger scale, a sumptuous autobiographical hymn to his rebirth through Krishna and the devotional obligations of that renewal. Many of the fifteen Harrison originals on the set were composed in 1969, as he struggled against the patronizing restrictions of writing within and for the Beatles. "My Sweet Lord," however, came to Harrison while he was on the road that December as a guest guitarist with Delaney and Bonnie. Inspired by the surprise 1969 gospel hit "Oh Happy Day" by the Edwin Hawkins Singers, Harrison started writing "My Sweet Lord" during a tour stop in Copenhagen, singing "Hallelujah" and "Hare Krishna" as he alternated between major and minor chords on a guitar. After the song's release as a single in November 1970, Harrison became embroiled in a dispiriting court case in which he was accused of pilfering three notes from the Chiffons' 1963 hit "He's So Fine" for "My Sweet Lord." But in its call-and-response structure and uplifting intent, "My Sweet Lord" was the honest child of black American sacred song, a psalm to Krishna that Harrison and his coproducer, Phil Spector, enriched with commercial sugar and ecumenical swing.

"If I were doing it now, it would not be so produced," Harrison said of *All Things Must Pass* in a ROLLING STONE interview when the set was reissued as a deluxe CD box in 2001. "But it was the first [solo] record, and I had Phil Spector helping me working on it. And anybody who's familiar with Phil's work–it was like Cinemascope sound. I think if I was doing it today, I would have less production. I did that on my next album, *Living in the Material World.* I dropped the big production and did it more like a small group." Indeed, Harrison returned to "My Sweet Lord" for that reissue, creating a bonus track–"My Sweet Lord (2000)"–in which he stripped Spector's Wall of Sound back to the original instrumental bed and recorded new percussion, guitars and vocals that emphasized the gospel origins of the song and underscored the humble certitude in Harrison's entreaty: "My sweet Lord–I really want to know you/I really want to go with you/I really want to show you Lord that it/Won't take long my Lord."

Harrison lost the "My Sweet Lord" case, brought against him by the estate of Ronnie Mack, the writer of "He's So Fine," and Bright Tunes, the song's publishers. After three days of testimony in February 1976, federal judge Richard Owen ruled that Harrison had committed "unconscious plagiarism." Harrison eventually paid damages of nearly six hundred thousand dollars. He also had his revenge. For his 1976 album, *Thirty-three and 1/3,* Harrison recorded a satirical gem simply called "This Song," in which he insisted that the melody was lawsuit-free: "This tune has nothing Bright about it/This tune ain't good or bad and come ever what may/My expert tells me it's okay."

Released as a single, "This Song" (featuring a spoken cameo by Eric Idle of the Monty Python comedy troupe) made it into *Billboard'*s Top Thirty. As an executive at Harrison's record company, Warner Bros., put it, "Harrison picked a mighty tough way to get a hit record."

ALL THOSE YEARS AGO
Written by George Harrison
Produced by George Harrison
and Ray Cooper

* Recorded in January 1981
* Released by George Harrison on
Somewhere in England in June 1981

IN 1980, George Harrison submitted a new solo album, *Somewhere in England,* to executives at Warner Bros. Records, the company that distributed his Dark Horse label. The suits handed it back, complaining that it was too downbeat. Then, on December 8, Harrison's former band mate, John Lennon, was murdered in front of his home at the Dakota in New York. Devastated by Lennon's death, Harrison turned to a song that he had recently composed for Ringo Starr to record. Rewritten and partly rerecorded, "All Those Years Ago" became the sentimental and melodic highlight of the amended *Somewhere* album and a kind of memorial gathering for Lennon: The finished track featured all three surviving Beatles.

The emotional exhaustion and financial acrimony that resulted in the breakup of the Beatles in 1970 have long obscured the fact that, throughout the next decade, they often appeared on one another's records, mostly helping Starr on his solo efforts. Harrison and Lennon, in particular, maintained a productive working relationship. Harrison played lead guitar on Lennon's 1970 agit-pop hit "Instant Karma" and provided the torrid slide work on Lennon's *Imagine,* heightening the argumentative energy of "Gimme Some Truth" and Lennon's attack on Paul McCartney, "How Do You Sleep?"

But "All Those Years Ago" was an exceptionally nostalgic song for Harrison, a man who rarely expressed fond memories of the Beatles, at least in public. Keeping the breezy instrumental track that Starr had taped in July 1980 for his own aborted solo album, *Can't Fight Lightning,* Harrison wrote new words in which he insisted his mixed feelings about the Beatles as a group never interfered with his admiration for Lennon's honesty and artistry: "Living with good and bad/I always looked up to you/Now we're left cold and sad/By someone/The devil's best friend/Someone who offended all." In a gesture of peace and common grief, Harrison invited Paul and Linda McCartney to sing background harmonies on the track atop Starr's original drums—a poignant reminder that, with Lennon gone, there could never be a true Beatles reunion. (The trio recorded again in the 1990s, over old Lennon demos, to create "new" Beatles music—without the magic—for the *Anthology 1* and *2* sets.)

"All Those Years Ago" became Harrison's biggest single in eight years, reaching Number Two on *Billboard'*s Top 100 chart. And he would revisit the weight and wonder of Beatlemania on his 1987 hit album, *Cloud Nine,* in the impressive *Sgt. Pepper* pastiche "When We Was Fab": "The microscope that magnified the tears/Studied warts and all/Still the life flowed on and on." In August 1966, as the Beatles returned to England after playing their last full concert together at Candlestick Park in San Francisco, Harrison famously snapped, "That's it. I'm not a Beatle anymore." But in the tender remembering of these songs, Harrison showed that, in his heart and art, he never left.

"The Beatles *are* a gas," Harrison declared in a 1974 British radio interview, emphasizing the present tense. And from that first recording session in Hamburg, Germany, until his final solo years, George Harrison sang his songs and played his guitar with nothing less than the passion and imagination of a Beatle. With quiet soul and diligent craft, he made living history.   ✳

A

COMPLETE

DISCOGRAPHY

BY
GREG
KOT

1961–1964

**TONY SHERIDAN AND
THE BEAT BROTHERS:**

"My Bonnie (Lies Over the Ocean)"/
"The Saints (When the Saints Go Marching In)"
single (released October 1961, Germany)
Mr. Twist EP (April 1962, France)
"Ya-Ya (Part 1 and 2)"/"Sweet Georgia Brown"
single (October 1962, Germany)
*The Beatles With Tony Sheridan and
Their Guests* (February 3, 1964)
The Beatles First (June 19, 1964, U.K.)

A SERIES OF German recordings from 1961 (later compiled on 1964 albums for U.S. and U.K. release) capture the Beatles as the toast of Hamburg's notorious Reeperbahn district at the Top Ten club. The Beatles–with Pete Best on drums, along with John Lennon, Paul McCartney and George Harrison–frequently perform with British expatriate singer Tony Sheridan at the Hamburg clubs and are signed to a deal by impresario Bert Kaempfert, who has them record mostly cheesy standards. A Harrison-Lennon instrumental, "Cry for a Shadow," with Harrison on lead guitar, debuts on the *Mr. Twist* EP.

Previous page: Recording 'A Hard Day's Night' in London at Abbey Road studios in 1964. Above: The Beatles rehearse for the "All You Need Is Love" broadcast, seen live by four hundred million viewers in twenty-four countries on June 25, 1967. For the show, the band's gear had psychedelic paint jobs. "It looked great, and it was just because we were tripping," recalled Paul McCartney. "Look at your guitar and you'd trip even more."

THE BEATLES

Please Please Me (March 22, 1963, U.K.)
Twist and Shout EP (July 12, 1963, U.K.)
The Beatles Hits EP (September 6, 1963, U.K.)
With the Beatles (November 22, 1963, U.K.;
November 25, 1963, Canada)

THE BEATLES lay the groundwork for their conquest of America on their first collaborations with producer George Martin. The songs on the U.K. debut album, *Please Please Me,* will surface on various U.S. releases, including *Introducing the Beatles* (1963), *Meet the Beatles* (1964), *The Early Beatles* (1965) and *Rarities* (1980). With "Don't Bother Me," Harrison breaks into the songwriting ranks on the second U.K. album, *With the Beatles* (which, like the first U.K. album, will be redistributed among several U.S. albums).

THE BEATLES

Meet the Beatles (January 20, 1964,
reached Number One on the *Billboard* chart)
Introducing the Beatles (July 22, 1963;
rereleased January 27, 1964, Number Two)
The Beatles' Second Album
(April 10, 1964, Number One)
A Hard Day's Night (June 26, 1964, Number One)
Something New (July 20, 1964, Number Two)
Beatles for Sale (December 4, 1964, U.K.)
Beatles '65 (December 15, 1964, Number One)

IN 1964, the year in which they burst onto the world's stage, the Beatles produce an astonishing six albums that reach either Number One or Two on the American pop charts. Harrison is a master of economy and restraint, a lead guitarist who embroiders the melody rather than his ego. His twangy fills and bebopping leads stamp him as a disciple of Carl Perkins, Chuck

Berry and Scotty Moore, never more so than on "I Saw Her Standing There" (from *Meet the Beatles*), where his reverb-drenched solo seems airmailed across the Atlantic from the Sun Records studio in Memphis. On these half-dozen albums, Harrison advances as a guitar player from a Perkins-Berry acolyte to a bold experimentalist; he is among the first musicians to experiment with the twelve-string Rickenbacker guitar and uses it extensively on *A Hard Day's Night*.

* * *

1965–1966

THE BEATLES

Beatles VI (June 14, 1965, Number One)
Help! (August 13, 1965, Number One)
Rubber Soul (December 6, 1965, Number One)
Yesterday and Today
(June 20, 1966, Number One)

THE BEATLES' GROWTH as songwriters and sonic craftsmen takes a quantum leap, with Lennon ("You've Got to Hide Your Love Away") and McCartney ("Yesterday") in peak form; Harrison advances markedly as a musician, pioneering the use of Eastern instruments in the pop world. The guitarist also steps up with more frequent and increasingly sophisticated songwriting contributions: "You Like Me Too Much" is uncharacteristically giddy, "I Need You" is notable primarily for the guitarist's experimentation with the volume pedal, "Think for Yourself" pits Harrison's complex chord changes against McCartney's fuzz-tone bass line, and "If I Needed Someone" is his finest tune to date, fusing the chiming Rickenbacker riff from the Byrds' "The Bells of Rhymney" with the guitarist's growing fascination with Indian music. That influence is also heard on Lennon's "Norwegian Wood," on which Harrison introduces the sitar to the rock lexicon.

* * *

THE BEATLES

Revolver
(August 8, 1966, Number One)

THE SAME YEAR they quit touring as a band, the Beatles make rock & roll a studio art form with this masterpiece. Harrison comes into his own as a songwriter, with two major contributions–"Taxman," an unusually direct rant (it names names in Britain's political establishment) built on one of Harrison's nastiest riffs; and "Love You Too," a boldly experimental track that Harrison records without his band mates as he makes the first full-scale incorporation of Eastern instruments on a Beatles album. *Revolver* also marks another first for Harrison: the inclusion of a third song, "I Want to Tell You."

* * *

1967

THE BEATLES

Sgt. Pepper's Lonely Hearts Club Band
(June 2, 1967, Number One)

INITIALLY DERIDED by some listeners as the low point on a landmark album, Harrison's cross-cultural fusion on "Within You Without You" is an ahead-of-its-time composition with blunt finger-pointing lyrics ("Are you one of them?"), a dreamy meditative drone and extensive Eastern instrumentation.

* * *

THE BEATLES

Magical Mystery Tour
(November 27, 1967, Number One)

HARRISON CONTRIBUTES one of his least-memorable Beatles tracks, "Blue Jay Way," a song essentially about boredom–and it sounds like it. The guitarist also cowrites the instrumental "Flying," the only composition credited to all four Beatles.

* * *

1968

THE BEATLES

The Beatles
(November 25, 1968, Number One)

HARRISON'S "While My Guitar Gently Weeps" is one of the enduring highlights of the Beatles' White Album. The tears on "Weeps" are wrenched from the guitar of Harrison's friend Eric Clapton, whose contribution is a dramatic departure from the overdriven blues sound of Cream, his group at the time. The antiestablishment commentary "Piggies" is too blunt to work as satire, and–save for its experimentation with some jazzy horn voicings–"Savoy Truffle" is indeed a trifle. But "Long, Long, Long" is quintessential Harrison, summarizing the impending

exhaustion of the Beatles and the era they defined, while pointing the way toward the spiritual heights achieved by his solo debut masterpiece, *All Things Must Pass*.

* * *

GEORGE HARRISON
Wonderwall Music soundtrack
(December 2, 1968, Number Forty-nine)

HARRISON'S INDIAN-INFLUENCED soundtrack for a movie set in swinging London.

* * *

1969
THE BEATLES
Yellow Submarine
(January 13, 1969, Number Two)

HARRISON HAS JOKED that "Only a Northern Song" was recorded simply to fill a contract obligation. But once again, a raga-flavored groove brings out Harrison's best in the walloping "It's All Too Much."

* * *

GEORGE HARRISON
Electronic Sounds
(May 26, 1969, Number 191)

HARRISON BECOMES ONE of the first rock musicians to dabble in electronic music, though the results are less than memorable.

* * *

THE BEATLES
Abbey Road
(September 26, 1969, Number One)

THE BEATLES' FINAL, troubled recording session yields two of Harrison's most elegant songs: the immortal "Something" and the simpler, but just as intoxicating, "Here Comes the Sun," which was composed in Eric Clapton's garden during a respite from a contentious Beatles business meeting. Harrison's acoustic-guitar intro is a song in itself, its warmth and fragility presaging the guarded optimism of the lyric.

* * *

1970
THE BEATLES
Hey Jude (The Beatles Again)
(February 26, 1970, Number Two)

RELEGATED TO THE B SIDE of Lennon's "The Ballad of John and Yoko" when it is released as a single in 1969,

the dark, droll, rollicking "Old Brown Shoe" resurfaces on *Hey Jude*. It may be Harrison's most underrated Beatles composition.

* * *

THE BEATLES
Let It Be
(May 8, 1970, Number One)

MCCARTNEY AND LENNON dismiss some of Harrison's most sophisticated compositions during the tumultuous sessions; many of these rejects will later surface in glorious form on *All Things Must Pass*. Lennon shows interest in playing only the simplest ditties, so Harrison presents "For You Blue," which amusingly invokes Elmore James during Lennon's bottleneck guitar solo, and "I Me Mine," a waltz-time rant against greed and selfishness.

* * *

GEORGE HARRISON
All Things Must Pass
(November 27, 1970, Number One)

THE BEATLES' LOSS is Harrison's gain. The guitarist had brought songs such as "All Things Must Pass," "Let It Down" and "Isn't It a Pity" to the Beatles in their fractious final months, only to have them rejected by Lennon and McCartney. Instead, they end up on this audacious coming-out party for the most self-effacing Beatle. Here is a twenty-three-song, three-album box set containing a who's who of the decade's rock royalty:

Ravi Shankar: "At first, 'Norwegian Wood,' to me, sounded so terrible. I had to keep my mouth shut."

Harrison's old Beatles running mates Ringo Starr and sideman Billy Preston, Eric Clapton and the future members of his group Derek and the Dominos, a nineteen-year-old pre-Genesis Phil Collins, Dave Mason and many others. Their efforts are orchestrated into a dense, echo-laden cathedral of rock in excelsis by Phil Spector, a producer famous for overwhelming his subjects. But the real stars of this monumental effort are Harrison's songs, which give awe-inspiring dimension to his spirituality and sobering depth to his yearning for a love that doesn't lie. Anchored by the pop hymn "My Sweet Lord," *All Things Must Pass* stands as one of the strongest solo recordings by any of the Beatles.

1971

THE CONCERT FOR BANGLA DESH

(December 20, 1971, Number Two)

HARRISON ORGANIZES a 1971 Madison Square Garden concert for famine relief in Bangladesh, a precursor to Live Aid and other all-star rock charity events. It results in a movie and a triple album. The performances also provide a snapshot of early-Seventies rock royalty, with Eric Clapton's guitar solo on "While My Guitar Gently Weeps," and a sharply focused five-song set by Bob Dylan.

* * *

1973

GEORGE HARRISON

Living in the Material World

(May 30, 1973, Number One)

MORE SONGS ABOUT THE RICHES of spirituality and the bankruptcy of materialism, without the mystical grandeur of *All Things Must Pass.* Harrison's signature slide guitar kicks "Give Me Love" to a higher plane and onto the pop charts, but the rest of the album is drearily monochromatic. "Who Can See It" and "The Day the World Gets 'Round" aspire to a hymnlike calm but never rise to the transcendent heights of Harrison's best work.

* * *

1974

GEORGE HARRISON

Dark Horse

(December 9, 1974, Number Four)

UNLIKE THE TIRED ARRANGEMENTS for *Living in the Material World,* Harrison's fifth solo album experiments with jazzier backdrops, employing jazz-funk band Tom Scott and the L.A. Express. But Harrison's voice is badly strained from tour rehearsals and it turns much of *Dark Horse* into an unintentionally comic exercise. The title song continues in the condescending autobiographical vein of such *Material World* tracks as "The Light That Has Lighted the World," declaring that "You thought that you knew where I was and when/But it looks like they've been foolin' you again."

1975

GEORGE HARRISON

Extra Texture

(Read All About It)

(September 22, 1975, Number Eight)

'EXTRA TEXTURE' IS SOMETHING of a return to form for Harrison, featuring such ruminative arrangements as "The Answer's at the End" and a terrific single, "You," originally intended for Ronnie Spector. Its roaring Wall of Sound arrangement suits Harrison well, right down to its closing quote of the Ronettes' "Be My Baby."

* * *

1976

GEORGE HARRISON

The Best of George Harrison

(November 8, 1976, Number Thirty-one)

A RETROSPECTIVE THAT DIVIDES Harrison's career between Beatles hits and early solo recordings.

* * *

GEORGE HARRISON

Thirty-three and 1/3

(November 24, 1976, Number Eleven)

"CRACKERBOX PALACE" HAS A TWINKLE in its eye, the kind of song that had previously eluded the increasingly self-serious Harrison as he tried to work out his post–*All Things Must Pass* blues. The tune's melodic sweep is nearly matched by "This Song," Harrison's sarcastic commentary on his "My Sweet Lord" plagiarism suit. The two tracks form the center of the guitarist's strongest collection since his solo debut.

* * *

1979

GEORGE HARRISON

George Harrison

(February 14, 1979, Number Fourteen)

"HERE COMES THE MOON" is a dreamy little wonder, the kind of incantation that underscores the romantic subtlety of Harrison's first album in three years. Misty-eyed and mellow in the wake of his marriage to Olivia Arias and the birth of his son, Dhani, Harrison is breezily ingratiating on "Blow Away" and "Faster."

The Traveling Wilburys (Bob "Lucky" Dylan, Tom "Charlie T. Jr." Petty, Jeff "Otis" Lynne, George "Nelson" Harrison, from left) began as an impromptu jam at Dylan's L.A. home and resulted in two platinum albums.

1981

GEORGE HARRISON

Somewhere in England

(June 1, 1981, Number Eleven)

NOT EVEN A FORMER BEATLE IS IMMUNE to record-industry machinations. Harrison's label, Warner Bros., rejects the artist's first attempt at *Somewhere in England.* He returns to the studio and writes the bitter "Blood From a Clone" in response but also comes up with "All Those Years Ago," a sprightly slice of Fab Four nostalgia that steers away from mourning John Lennon's recent death and instead celebrates the Bea-tles' beginnings. The track also reunites Harrison with Starr and McCartney in the studio, the last time they would record together until the 1995 reunion.

* * *

1982

GEORGE HARRISON

Gone Troppo

(October 27, 1982, Number 108)

THE ICY KEYBOARDS and unusually theatrical singing on "Wake Up My Love," the doo-wop vocals on "I Really Love You" and Harrison's experimentation with synthesizers suggest that the guitarist is trying to shake up the formula, but today *Gone Troppo* sounds dated, burdened by glossy Eighties pop-rock production touches.

* * *

1985

GEORGE HARRISON

Porky's Revenge! soundtrack
(March 14, 1985, Number 122)

CONTINUING THEIR LOOSE long-running partnership, Harrison performs Dylan's "I Don't Want to Do It."

* * *

GREENPEACE

(August 19, 1985)

HARRISON CONTRIBUTES a remixed "Save the World" to this charity compilation.

* * *

GEORGE HARRISON

Water soundtrack (June 28, 1985)

HARRISON PERFORMS and cowrites this soundtrack to a HandMade Films Michael Caine vehicle.

* * *

1987

GEORGE HARRISON

Songs by George Harrison (1987)

A LIMITED-EDITION DISC featuring previously unreleased gems including "Lay His Head" and "Sat Singing."

* * *

GEORGE HARRISON

Cloud Nine
(November 2, 1987, Number Eight)

HARRISON SOUNDS REENERGIZED collaborating with producer and Beatles fanatic Jeff Lynne and a band that includes Eric Clapton on guitar, Elton John on keyboards and Ringo Starr on drums. Harrison has rarely sounded as punchy as he does on "Fish on the Sand," "Devil's Radio," "This Is Love" and on his cover of James Ray's 1962 hit "Got My Mind Set on You," while "Just for Today" achieves a radiant stateliness. "When We Was Fab" is an affectionate, Rutles-like parody of Harrison's old band and its kaleidoscopic *Sgt. Pepper*-era studio adventures. The blazing smile Harrison sports on the cover says it all: The guitarist has never sounded like he was having more fun in the studio.

1988

THE TRAVELING WILBURYS

The Traveling Wilburys (Volume One)
(October 25, 1988, Number Three)

HARRISON IS JOINED BY Bob Dylan, Roy Orbison, Tom Petty and Jeff Lynne for kicks and giggles. *The Traveling Wilburys (Volume One)* is almost a parody of a supergroup that nonetheless becomes a major commercial success. A scruffy informality prevails: The five gather in Dylan's garage rehearsal space for a series of casual jams, and the Saturday-night breeziness of the affair seems to refresh Dylan in particular, who has rarely sounded this frisky on record. The album also serves as a fitting final showcase for rock legend Orbison, who dies six weeks after the Wilburys' debut is released. Among the highlights are a prototypical Orbison ballad, "Not Alone Anymore," and a rambling, tongue-in-cheek Dylan narrative, "Tweeter and the Monkey Man," that counters his late-Eighties songwriting malaise. The democratic setting particularly suits Harrison, whose supportive inclinations as a slide guitarist, harmony vocalist and coproducer give the project a seamlessness that belies the disparate styles and tender egos involved.

* * *

1989

GEORGE HARRISON

The Best of Dark Horse (1976–1989)
(October 1989)

A FIFTEEN-TRACK COLLECTION that covers the years from *Thirty-three and 1/3* to *Cloud Nine.*

* * *

1990

THE TRAVELING WILBURYS

The Traveling Wilburys (Volume Three)
(October 30, 1990, Number Eleven)

EVEN MORE SO than on *Volume One,* the Wilburys—now reduced to a foursome of Harrison, Dylan, Lynne and Petty—find a common vernacular in the rock & roll of the Fifties and early Sixties. An ingratiating goofiness reigns on "Cool Dry Place," "Inside Out," "Poor House" and "Wilbury Twist." The Marcels' doo-wop hit "Blue Moon" is redone as "7 Deadly Sins" and also as a calypso, "New Blue Moon." As on *Volume One,* Harrison is again listed as coproducer with Lynne.

1992
GEORGE HARRISON
Live in Japan
(July 14, 1992, Number 126)

HARRISON TOURS FOR THE FIRST TIME since 1974, backed by Eric Clapton and his band. The former Beatle surveys his entire career on these two discs: Though superfluous backing harmonies nearly capsize "While My Guitar Gently Weeps," Clapton resurrects it with a pair of sighing, ringing solos, and a hopped-up cover of Chuck Berry's "Roll Over Beethoven" returns Harrison to his Hamburg nightclub days with the Beatles.

* * *

1994
THE BEATLES
Live at the BBC
(December 1994, Number Three)

THIS TWO-DISC OVERVIEW of the tracks the Beatles recorded for the British Broadcasting Corp. from 1962 to '65 illuminates the quartet's facility as a live working band, tackling a huge stylistic range of material with one-take alacrity. Harrison's guitar playing has a pronounced twang, reflecting his love of rockabilly, but his choice of chords also reflects an undeniable jazz sensibility. By the time of "I Feel Fine" in 1964, Harrison and Lennon are picking out a complex, syncopated blues riff in unison that is well beyond just about anything heard in pop at the time.

* * *

1995
THE BEATLES
Anthology 1
(November 21, 1995, Number One)

THE SURVIVING BEATLES kick off their massive *Anthology* campaign—devoted to previously unreleased studio rarities and outtakes from the Sixties—with their first new single in twenty-five years, "Free as a Bird." Though the tune lacks the zest of the band's best singles, it has a sweet, dreamy glow—Harrison's achingly eloquent slide-guitar solo is the song's crowning moment. *Anthology 1* includes "Cry for a Shadow," a jazzy 1961 instrumental that was Harrison's first Beatles composing credit, shared with Lennon. Another curiosity is an early unfinished Harrison track, "You Know What to Do," performed with little more than a guitar and a tambourine.

1996
THE BEATLES
Anthology 2
(March 19, 1996, Number One)

A SECOND RESURRECTED LENNON demo is transformed into another "new" Beatles single, "Real Love," which, like "Free as a Bird," is distinguished by Harrison's lyrical guitar work. Also included are early takes of "Norwegian Wood" and "Within You Without You" that reiterate the pronounced Eastern flavor Harrison brings to the group with his use of Indian instrumentation.

* * *

THE BEATLES
Anthology 3
(October 29, 1996, Number One)

'ANTHOLOGY 3' DOCUMENTS the Beatles' final years and Harrison's arrival as a first-rate songwriter. Most im-pressive are the acoustic demos for the White Album, in particular Harrison's beautiful solo version of "While My Guitar Gently Weeps," as well as pristine early takes on "Something" and "Piggies." Harrison's stinging, electrified "Not Guilty," however, has to wait until the guitarist's 1979 release, *George Harrison,* before it appears on album.

* * *

2000
THE BEATLES
1
(November 14, 2000, Number One)

THE BEATLES MARK THEIR FIFTH DECADE on the pop charts with an immaculate collection of twenty-seven blockbusters, including "Something."

* * *

2001
GEORGE HARRISON
All Things Must Pass rerelease
(January 23, 2001)

A RERELEASE OF HARRISON'S finest work on its thirtieth anniversary, with especially worthy bonus tracks such as the countrified "I Live for You," with a fine pedal-steel solo by the late Pete Drake, and a tart demo of "Beware of Darkness." ❀

OTHER RECORDINGS

Side projects, guest appearances and production work

BY GREG KOT

with REPORTING *by*
URANIA MYLONAS *and* JASON STUTTS

CREAM
Goodbye
(March 1969, Number Two)
Harrison returns the favor for
Eric Clapton's guest appearance
on the Beatles' "While My Guitar
Gently Weeps," cowriting and
playing rhythm guitar on "Badge."

* * *

JACKIE LOMAX
Is This What You Want?
(May 19, 1969, Number 145)
BILLY PRESTON
*That's the Way God
Planned It* (September 10,
1969, Number 127)
DORIS TROY
Doris Troy (November 9, 1970)
RONNIE SPECTOR
"Try Some, Buy Some"/"Tan-
doori Chicken" single (April 19,
1971, Number Seventy-seven)
RADHA KRISHNA TEMPLE
Radha Krishna Temple
(May 21, 1971)
**LON AND DERREK
VAN EATON**
Brother (March 6, 1972)
Among Harrison's first produc-
ing credits are recordings by
Ronnie Spector and five other
acts signed to Apple Records:
Beatles sideman Preston, Liver-

pool crony Lomax, soul
singer Troy, the Van Eaton
duo and a group of London-
based Krishna devotees.

* * *

JACK BRUCE
Songs for a Tailor (October 6,
1969, Number Fifty-five)
JOHN LENNON
"Instant Karma (We All Shine
On)" single (February 20,
1970, Number Three)
LEON RUSSELL
Leon Russell (March 23,
1970, Number Sixty)
BILLY PRESTON
Encouraging Words (November 9,
1970); *I Wrote a Simple Song*
(November 8, 1971,
Number Thirty-two); *It's
My Pleasure* (July 20, 1975,
Number Forty-three)
GARY WRIGHT
Footprint (November 1, 1971)
**JOHN LENNON
AND YOKO ONO**
Some Time in New York City
(June 12, 1972, Number Forty-eight)
HARRY NILSSON
Son of Schmilsson (July 10,
1972, Number Twelve); *Son of
Dracula* soundtrack (April 1,
1974, Number 106)

NICKY HOPKINS
The Tin Man Was a Dreamer
(April 23, 1973, Number 108)
DAVE MASON
It's Like You Never Left
(October 29, 1973, Number Fifty)
**ALVIN LEE AND
MYLON LEFEVRE**
On the Road to Freedom
(November 2, 1973, Number 138)
DAVID BROMBERG
Wanted Dead or Alive
(January 7, 1974, Number 167)
TOM SCOTT
New York Connection
(August 25, 1975, Number
Forty-two)
LARRY HOSFORD
Cross Words (1976)
Harrison, sometimes hiding
behind pseudonyms such as
Hari Georgeson, plays sideman
on these recordings by
his pals. His tunes "My Sweet
Lord" and "All Things Must
Pass" make their debut on
Preston's *Encouraging Words*,
weeks before his own *All
Things Must Pass* comes out.

* * *

JAMES TAYLOR
"Carolina in My Mind"
single (October 26, 1970,

With Badfinger's Pete Ham, Apple Studios, 1971

Number Sixty-seven)
Harrison sings harmony on
one of the folk singer's early
singles, for Apple.

* * *

RINGO STARR
"It Don't Come Easy" single
(April 16, 1971, Number Four)
Harrison produced and may
have cowritten this single.

* * *

JOHN LENNON
Imagine (September 9,
1971, Number One)
Harrison contributes dobro and
slide guitar on three songs.

* * *

RAVI SHANKAR
Raga soundtrack (December 7,
1971); *In Concert 1972* (January 22,
1973); *Shankar Family and
Friends* (October 7, 1974, Number

176); *Ravi Shankar's Music Festival From India* (February 6,
1976); *In Celebration* four-CD
set (December 5, 1995)
Harrison produced three albums
and a box set for his sitar-playing
mentor from India.

* * *

BADFINGER
Straight Up (December 13,
1971, Number Thirty-one)
Harrison coproduces and plays
lead guitar on "Day After Day,"
a Number Four hit single for
the Apple Records band.

* * *

RINGO STARR
"Back Off Boogaloo"
single (March 20, 1972,
Number Nine)
Harrison produced
and played guitar.

ERIC CLAPTON
History of Eric Clapton
(April 10, 1972, Number Six)
In addition to the Harrison-
Clapton tune "Badge," this
anthology includes "Tell the
Truth," to which Harrison
contributes a bristling solo.

* * *

THE BEATLES
The Beatles: 1962–1966 (April 20,
1973, Number Three); *The Beatles:
1967–1970* (April 20, 1973, Number
One); *Rock and Roll Music* (June
11, 1976, Number Two); *The Beatles at the Hollywood Bowl* (May
6, 1977, Number Two); *The Beatles
Live! At the Star-Club in Hamburg, Germany* (June 13, 1977,
Number 111); *Love Songs* (October
21, 1977, Number Twenty-four);
Rarities (March 24, 1980, Number

Twenty-one); *Reel Music* (March 12, 1982, Number Nineteen) A few relatively obscure Harrison gems resurface amid a long line of successful Beatles compilations, repackagings and live recordings: *Rock and Roll Music* resurrects the manic 1965 B side "I'm Down," with McCartney's throat-shredding vocal equaled by Harrison's biting guitar solo; and *Rarities* unearths the 1968 "Lady Madonna" B side, "The Inner Light," another of Harrison's raga tracks recorded with Indian musicians.

* * *

CHEECH AND CHONG

Los Cochinos (August 27, 1973, Number Two) Yes, that's Harrison's guitar on the immortal "Basketball Jones Featuring Tyrone Shoelaces."

* * *

RINGO STARR

Ringo (November 2, 1973, Number Two) Harrison cowrites the hit "Photograph" and other tunes, plays guitar and sings harmonies.

* * *

SPLINTER

The Place I Love (September 25, 1974, Number Eighty-one); *Harder to Live* (October 6, 1975); *Two Man Band* (October 3, 1977) Harrison produced and played on these albums recorded by a band he recruited for his Dark Horse label.

* * *

RON WOOD

I've Got My Own Album to Do (1974) Harrison sings, shares writing credit

and creates his characteristic sound on the enjoyable "Far East Man," which also appeared simultaneously on Harrison's *Dark Horse*.

* * *

RINGO STARR

Goodnight Vienna (November 18, 1974, Number Eight); *Blast From Your Past* (November 20, 1975, Number Thirty); *Ringo's Rotogravure* (1976, Number Twenty-eight) Harrison wrote the track "I'll Still Love You" on *Rotogravure*, and the Harrison-Starr hit "Photograph" is included on the *Blast From Your Past* compilation.

* * *

MONTY PYTHON

"Lumberjack Song" single (November 14, 1975); "The Pirate Song" single (1976, U.K.); "Always Look on the Bright Side of Life" single (October 14, 1975) In addition to bankrolling Monty Python movies, Harrison cowrote "The Pirate Song" with Eric Idle, produced "Lumberjack Song" and helped mix "Always Look on the Bright Side."

* * *

DARYL HALL AND JOHN OATES

Along the Red Ledge (September 29, 1978, Number Twenty-seven) "The Last Time" features Harrison on slide guitar.

* * *

DUANE EDDY

Duane Eddy (1979); *His Twangy Guitar and the Rebels* (1995) Harrison pays tribute to

one of his guitar idols with some slide guitar.

* * *

RINGO STARR

Stop and Smell the Roses (October 27, 1981) Harrison wrote the lead single, "Wrack My Brain."

* * *

GEORGE HARRISON

Time Bandits film score (1981) Harrison's original score for this HandMade Films production was never released as an album, although the closing song, "Dream Away," can be found on *Gone Troppo*.

* * *

MICK FLEETWOOD

The Visitor (1981, Number Forty-three) The ex-Beatle contributes guitar and vocals to "Walk a Thin Line."

* * *

GARY BROOKER

Lead Me to the Water (1982) Harrison plays guitar on "Mineral Man."

* * *

ALVIN LEE

Detroit Diesel (1986, Number 124); *Zoom* (1992); *Nineteen Ninetyfour* (April 13, 1995) Harrison contributes slide guitar to various album tracks by the former Ten Years After frontman.

* * *

SYLVIA GRIFFIN

Love's a State of Mind (1988)

JIM CAPALDI

Some Come Running (1988, Number 183) Harrison delivers guitar and slide-guitar cameos.

ROY ORBISON

Mystery Girl
(January 30, 1989, Number Five)
Harrison plays acoustic guitar
on "A Love So Beautiful."

* * *

TOM PETTY

Full Moon Fever
(April 29, 1989, Number Three)
Harrison sings backup vocals
and plays acoustic guitar on
"I Won't Back Down."

* * *

BELINDA CARLISLE

Runaway Horses
(1989, Number Thirty-seven)
Harrison plays six-string bass,
acoustic and slide guitar.

* * *

ERIC CLAPTON

Journeyman (November 1989,
Number Sixteen)
Harrison wrote a song for this album, "Run So Far," on which he
also sings and plays.

* * *

GARY MOORE

Still Got the Blues (May 1990,
Number Eighty-three)
Harrison sings and plays guitar on
"The Woman."

* * *

THE JEFF HEALEY BAND

Hell to Pay (May 29, 1990,
Number Twenty-seven)
Harrison sings backup vocals and
plays acoustic guitar on a cover of
"While My Guitar Gently Weeps."

* * *

JEFF LYNNE

Armchair Theatre
(1990, Number Eighty-three)
Harrison plays and sings on a number of songs, including "Every Little Thing" and "Lift Me Up."

BOB DYLAN

Under the Red Sky
(September 11, 1990,
Number Thirty-eight)
That's Harrison playing
slide on the title track.

* * *

**NOBODY'S CHILD:
ROMANIAN ANGEL APPEAL**

(October 17, 1990)
This benefit compilation features
Paul Simon and Harrison's duet of
Simon and Garfunkel's "Home-
ward Bound," from a performance
on *Saturday Night Live.*

* * *

BOB DYLAN

*The Bootleg Series, Volumes
1–3 (Rare and Unreleased)
1961–1991* (1991)
A 1970 version of Dylan's "If Not
for You," on which Harrison plays
guitar, finally sees release.

* * *

JIMMY NAIL

Growing Up in Public
(June 1992)
Harrison plays guitar on
"Real Love."

* * *

BOB DYLAN

*The 30th Anniversary
Concert Celebration*
(August 24, 1993)
Harrison sings lead vocals
on "Absolutely Sweet Marie,"
and plays guitar and sings
backup on "Knockin' on Heaven's
Door" and "My Back Pages."

* * *

CARL PERKINS

Go Cat Go!
(October 15, 1996)
Harrison honors Perkins's huge
influence on the Beatles by produc-

ing, playing guitar and bass
and singing on "Distance Makes
No Difference With Love."

* * *

RAVI SHANKAR

Chants of India
(May 6, 1997)
Produced by Harrison, who
also contributes guitar, bass,
glockenspiel, vibraphone,
autoharp and marimba as
well as backing vocals.

* * *

RINGO STARR

Vertical Man
(June 16, 1998)
George plays lead guitar on
"King of Broken Hearts" and
"I'll Be Fine Everywhere."

* * *

RUBYHORSE

How Far Have You Come?
(September 2000)
Harrison plays slide on the
track "Punchdrunk."

* * *

**ELECTRIC LIGHT
ORCHESTRA**

Zoom (June 12, 2001)
Harrison plays slide guitar
on "A Long Time Gone"
and "All She Wanted."

* * *

**BILL WYMAN'S
RHYTHM KINGS**

Double Bill (June 26, 2001)
Harrison contributes guitar
on "Love Letters."

* * *

JOOLS HOLLAND

Small World Big Band
(November 19, 2001, U.K.)
Harrison and his son, Dhani,
co-composed the song "Horse
to the Water."

The

MUSIC

25

*** ***

ESSENTIAL
HARRISON
PERFORMANCES

By DAVID FRICKE

"I SAW HER
STANDING THERE"
1963

GEORGE HARRISON'S IMMENSE contribution to rock & roll guitar starts here. Half of the single (with "I Want to Hold Your Hand") that fired the Beatles to Number One in America in February 1964, "I Saw Her Standing There" features Harrison's first guitar solo on an official Beatles release, recorded on February 11, 1963, during the daylong session that yielded the bulk of the British LP *Please Please Me*. Harrison's tightly wound phrases are dunked in cavelike echo and set in a growling register, an ingenious contrast to the high-pitched vocals of John Lennon and Paul McCartney.

* * *

"SHE LOVES YOU"
1963

HARRISON'S GRETSCH Country Gentleman punctuates the frantic vocal magic with big, rippled chords and choked-riff interjections bearing strong traces of Chuck Berry. Harrison's most memorable contribution, however, is his closing chord, played under the last "Yeah!" Producer George Martin recalled hearing the Beatles run through the song on acoustic guitars at the July 1, 1963, session: "I thought it was great but was intrigued by the final chord, an odd sort of major sixth . . . like a Glenn Miller arrangement." It became the unorthodox icing on the Beatles' first million-selling single.

* * *

"DON'T BOTHER ME"
1963

THE FIRST HARRISON SONG to appear on a Beatles album–*With the Beatles* in Britain; 1964's *Meet the Beatles* in America–is also Harrison's first song about suffocating celebrity. Written on tour in August 1963, while Harrison was bedridden with illness in a hotel, "Don't Bother Me" is, on the surface, about getting over a departed lover. But Harrison italicizes his real sense of loss ("I know I'll never be the same") with a brief fierce solo that sounds like he's spitting nails through his guitar.

* * *

"CAN'T BUY ME LOVE"
1964

THE BEATLES RUSHED through "Can't Buy Me Love" in a Paris studio on January 29, 1964, on a day off of sorts from a three-week grind of shows at the city's Olympia Theater. Harrison added his guitar solo a month later, on February 25, at EMI's Abbey Road studios. He repeatedly spears the same note. But double-tracking, with one take a hair out of phase with the other, gives the break a unique watery quality, as if it's coming from a wobbly old Sun Records 45.

* * *

"A HARD DAY'S NIGHT"
1964

OUTTAKES OF THE BEATLES working on the title song from their first feature film show Harrison fighting his way to excellence: jabbing at half-formed ideas, even fumbling notes, on his twelve-string Rickenbacker. But by 10:00 p.m. on April 16, 1964, after a three-hour session at Abbey Road, Harrison had made this Lennon-written raver his own: with his harmonic rain in the opening chord; the pearly ring of his guitar in the circular fade-out; and that solo, an ascending run of notes with a runaround flourish, doubled on piano by George Martin.

* * *

"EVERYBODY'S TRYING
TO BE MY BABY"
1964

THE BEATLES COVERED more songs by Carl Perkins than by any other artist, and they played this Harrison vocal specialty–taken from Perkins's 1958 Sun LP, *Dance Album for Carl Perkins*–the most, from 1961 to 1965. Skip the one-take version on *Beatles for Sale*. The November '64 blitz on *Live at the BBC* finds Harrison emulating Perkins, his top guitar hero, with concentrated flair. Harrison packs his Tennessee-farmhouse picking with Merseyside snarl, and the tumble of chords at the end of his first solo is a minimalist thrill.

"YES IT IS"
1965

A YEAR BEFORE THE BEATLES uncorked the mind-bending wonders of backward-tape recording, Harrison fell in love with the reverselike sustain of the volume pedal, a kind of proto wah-wah. He got that sound manually on 1964's "Baby's in Black"; Lennon turned the volume knob on Harrison's Gretsch Tennessean as he played. Harrison employed an actual pedal on his own "I Need You" in February 1965, then used it again the very next day on "Yes It Is," putting a subtle Nashville spin on Lennon's ballad with gentle sobs of pedal-steel-like guitar–three years before the advent of country rock.

* * *

"HELP!"
1965

T HE LYRIC WAS AS GOOD THEN as it is now," Lennon said of "Help!" in his 1970 ROLLING STONE interview. "It was just me singing 'help,' and I meant it." The title song of the Beatles' second movie was bristling autobiography, but Harrison's guitar fills in the chorus, appended to the twelfth and final take on April 13, 1965, answer Lennon's desperation with reverberant elegance: booming triplets that hang in the mix like heavy beads of sweat, followed by a warm spray of arpeggios that bathe the song in rays of hope.

* * *

"NORWEGIAN WOOD (THIS BIRD HAS FLOWN)"
1965

H ARRISON DISCOVERED THE SITAR in the spring of 1965 while shooting a scene in *Help!* with several Indian musicians. By mid-October, he was playing a sitar on this *Rubber Soul* waltz. His part merely echoes Lennon's vocal melody. But with this self-taught performance, Harrison introduced the instrument to the Beatles' audience while initiating his own lifelong passion for the sitar and its twentieth-century master, Ravi Shankar. The Beatles recorded the song at the first *Rubber Soul* session on October 12 but redid it on Oc-

Harrison with his Epiphone Casino, used on 'Revolver' in 1966. "I wouldn't say that my songs are autobiographical," Harrison said. "The early ones were just any words I could think of."

tober 21 because of difficulties in capturing the sitar's sharp, buzzing timbre on tape.

* * *

"DRIVE MY CAR"
1965

T HIS SONG IS NOTABLE for two things: It was recorded at the first Beatles session to run past midnight (12:15 a.m. on October 14, 1965); graveyard shifts would be the norm after this. Also, "Drive My Car" is as tight in its lock-step rhythm as anything that came out of Motown or Memphis that year. The Rolling Stones were considered the blacker band for their blues chops, but the doubling here of McCartney's bass and Harrison's throaty guitar shows the heavy soul in the Beatles' sound. The rubbery whine of Harrison's solo implies that he played it with a beer-bottle neck; actually, it was a tape-speed trick.

* * *

"IF I NEEDED SOMEONE"
1965

I N 1964, BYRDS GUITARIST Jim McGuinn–now Roger–bought a twelve-string Rickenbacker after seeing Harrison play one in *A Hard Day's Night*. By 1965, the Byrds were the Beatles' first serious American competition; the bands were also friends and an inspiration to each other. For this folk-rock diamond, recorded in October 1965, Harrison adapted his riff from McGuinn's lick in the Byrds' "The Bells of Rhymney," then sent the Byrds an advance copy of the track with a thank-you note: "This is for Jim."

* * *

"NOWHERE MAN"
1965

T HE UNISON CHIME of Fender Stratocasters, played by Harrison and Lennon, provides the sunshine in this confessional gem, written by Lennon in the third person about his own frustrations with Beatle life. Harrison had craved a Strat for years; he nearly bought one in Hamburg, Germany, in 1962 but was beaten to it by a member of Rory Storm and the Hurricanes. Harrison finally got a Strat in '65 and started playing it all over Beatles recordings. The melody in this break is surely a Harrison invention; it has his mark of luxuriant pith. Note, too, the glassy class of his single harmonic ping at the end.

"AND YOUR BIRD CAN SING"
1966

THE BEATLES FIRST ATTEMPTED this *Revolver* number on April 20, 1966, then entirely recut it on April 26. The difficulty the band had in establishing a balance between the song's folk-rock air and its brusque lead guitars was evident in Lennon's droll count-off at the start of the second session: "Okay, boys, quite brisk, *moderato,* fox trot." Nevertheless, Harrison navigates his harmonized, rococo guitar vamp with breezy aplomb.

* * *

"TAXMAN"
1966

HARRISON LANDED the plum spot on *Revolver*–side one, track one–with this sarcastic rebuttal to British tax rates. And rightly so: Harrison's psych-garage cruncher is a crucial, often overlooked bridge between the Beatles' straight quartet sound and their first dives into LSD-fried pop. McCartney plays the screeching-raga guitar solo, but the eccentric force of the song is in Harrison's hydraulic-R&B rhythm guitar, which future Mods the Jam hijacked with love for their 1980 U.K. hit "Start!"

* * *

"I'M ONLY SLEEPING"
1966

TO HARRISON, psychedelic guitar was not just a matter of peeling off a wigged-out solo and running the tape backward to approximate the mystical whoosh of the acid state. For this Lennon meditation on somnolent bliss, created over four days for *Revolver,* Harrison spent the third–May 5, 1966, from 9:30 p.m. until three the next morning–composing a solo he literally recorded backward, playing George Martin's reverse transcription of the notes. The tape was then run backward, or forward in the case of the solo itself. Harrison actually taped two solos, superimposed on each other for extra-drowsy effect.

* * *

"WITHIN YOU WITHOUT YOU"
1967

FORGET THE INDIAN MUSIC and listen to the melody," McCartney once remarked about another Harrison Indo-pop song, "The Inner Light." The same should be said of Harrison's sole composition on *Sgt. Pepper's*

Lonely Hearts Club Band, his purest excursion on a Beatles record into raga. Harrison's sitar solo in the middle actually sings and swings with the clarity and phrasing of his best rockabilly-fired guitar work. The entire song, in fact, can be played on the guitar with transportive force: Sonic Youth recorded an impressive version for a 1988 *Sgt. Pepper* tribute album.

* * *

"IT'S ALL TOO MUCH"
1967

WRITTEN BY HARRISON while flying on LSD, this psychedelic romp–vocal and instrumental anarchy atop a pulsing drone–evolved over three days as the Beatles rush-recorded new songs in the late spring of '67 for the cartoon fable *Yellow Submarine.* "George Harrison was in charge of the session," recalled trumpeter David Mason, who played on the track. "I don't think he really knew what he wanted." Harrison just piled on a feast of distorted Harrison-Lennon guitars and long peals of feedback clearly inspired by Britain's overnight sensation of that season: Jimi Hendrix.

* * *

"EVERYBODY'S GOT
SOMETHING TO HIDE
EXCEPT FOR
ME AND MY MONKEY"
1968

THE BEATLES SPENT TWO DAYS–June 26 and 27, 1968–on this White Album explosion of blistering guitars and barking vocals. And that was just to get the rhythm track right. The song is a Lennon salute to the joys of 1950s rock & roll animalism. But its locomotive heart is Harrison's whirl-around guitar figure, played with ferocious attitude against Lennon's crisp strum and the incessant clang of a hand bell.

* * *

"WHILE MY GUITAR
GENTLY WEEPS"
1968

ERIC CLAPTON PLAYED the magnificently pained electric solo on the White Album reading of this doleful classic; Harrison plays only acoustic guitar. He first taped the song, however, as a solo demo (with discreet McCartney organ) on July 25, 1968. Available on *Anthology 3* with an extra verse that didn't make it to the White Album, that performance has its own heart-stopping melancholy–a whispered admission of distress by a man who identifies so closely with his instrument that it shares his hurt.

* * *

"I WANT YOU (SHE'S SO HEAVY)"
1969

THE BEATLES' FIRST STAB at Lennon's half-Latin, half-metal blues took place at their own Apple Studios on January 29, 1969, the day before their performance on Apple's rooftop. But Harrison and Lennon didn't pour on their guitars until early on April 19, back at Abbey Road. Harrison contributes the cat's-meow fills and chiming arpeggios. The huge fun, though, is in hearing so much Lennon-and-Harrison guitar at once amid the white noise from Harrison's Moog synthesizer–played by Lennon.

* * *

"SOMETHING"
1969

LENNON SAID THIS HARRISON BALLAD was the best song on *Abbey Road.* Much of its majesty comes from the way Harrison colors his sentiments with rapturous guitars. The arrangement, developed between February and August 1969, is a tribute to Harrison's orchestral gifts–and perfectionist streak. Rejecting a previous solo, he cut another at the last session on August 15, live with the strings. His blend of bluesy grace and concise melody was "almost the same solo [as before]–note for note," says engineer Geoff Emerick. "The only reason I feel he wanted to redo it was emotion."

* * *

"I ME MINE"
1970

IT'S ABOUT THE EGO, the eternal problem," Harrison said of his song, the last new number recorded by the Beatles–on January 3, 1970–before their breakup in April. Only three Beatles showed up for work; Lennon was vacationing in Denmark. There wasn't much of a song, either: a mix of waltz-tempo and hot-boogie segments, running a minute and a half. (Producer Phil Spector stretched the track by repeating the first verse.) But Harrison signed off in style; his angry,

grinding guitar is the honest sound of exhaustion and hard-won freedom.

* * *

"MY SWEET LORD"
1970

THE EMPHASIS on prayer and transcendence in Harrison's solo records–particularly on this Number One single from his 1970 debut, *All Things Must Pass*–obscures the pivotal subtlety of his guitar playing. In 1971, Harrison was accused of cribbing three notes from the Chiffons' "He's So Fine" for "My Sweet Lord." (He lost the case in 1976.) Yet the defining charm of Harrison's hit is his silvery shots of dobrolike guitar, which pierce the creamy grandeur of Spector's coproduction like cries of country-blues joy.

* * *

"WHAT IS LIFE"
1970

HARRISON WROTE THIS EXULTANT SONG of surrender for Apple Records act Billy Preston but wisely kept it for *All Things Must Pass.* Spector matches the galloping rhythm with echo-drenched theater: brass, strings and a choir of multitracked Harrisons. The real ignition, though, is Harrison's pumping fuzz guitar in the intro and knockout choruses. "As a kid, I used to sing harmonies with my mom in the car to Harrison songs like 'What Is Life,' " says Dave Grohl, ex-Nirvana drummer and head Foo Fighter. That singalong magnetism sent this single into the Top Ten.

* * *

"GIVE ME LOVE (GIVE ME PEACE ON EARTH)"
1973

HARRISON'S SECOND Number One single in America was a soft, intimate hymn, a small-combo reaction to the Wagnerian spectacle of *All Things Must Pass.* Harrison's guitar is characteristically sweet and direct: the beaming harmony of doubled slide. "Gandhi says create and preserve the image of your choice," Harrison told ROLLING STONE in 1974. Within the Beatles and after, Harrison imagined himself not as a star but as a musician, a man of questions and expressive craft. That image is preserved in these songs and performances for all time.

✳

ADVENTURES

·ONSCREEN·

BY ADAM
DAWTREY

WHEN GEORGE
Harrison stood up to speak at the tenth-anniversary party of HandMade Films in 1988, the last thing that anyone was expecting from the shyest of the Beatles was an outburst of anger that would ultimately tear the company apart.

Around two hundred members of the British film industry were present at the gala dinner, which took place on two soundstages at Shepperton Studios in West London, where so many of HandMade's classic movies were shot.

They were there to celebrate the remarkable achievements of the company that Harrison and his American manager, Denis O'Brien, had launched a decade earlier, when they stepped in to bankroll *Monty Python's Life of Brian* after the original backers lost their nerve.

Artistic boldness was HandMade's hallmark. Even though Harrison left the day-to-day running to O'Brien and to the head of development, Ray Cooper, their willingness to gamble on the quirky, the unexpected and the downright eccentric reflected Harrison's own tastes. His sense of humor was closely aligned with the dark, subversive comedy that was HandMade's particular specialty.

This paid off with some of the most extraordinary, influential movies in the canon of British cinema. *Life of Brian* was followed by such indie classics as *Time Bandits, Mona Lisa* and *Withnail and I*, as well as *A Private Function, How to Get Ahead in Advertising* and *The Long Good Friday*. If Harrison had not already won greater fame as a rock legend, his career as a movie producer alone would have earned him a decent niche in the entertainment hall of fame. Rockers from Mick Jagger to Michael Stipe have followed Harrison's lead in the film-producing game. His presence at HandMade may have been intermittent, but he was regarded with enormous affection by the filmmakers (who conversely loathed O'Brien as a meddling bean counter) and the staff. Never the arrogant rock star, Harrison gave nothing but appreciation and encouragement—and, of course, his money—to underwrite the movies.

No one knows exactly what made him snap on the night of the tenth anniversary. He had seemed happy earlier that day, enthusiastically helping out with the preparations. He had arranged for his friend Carl Perkins to perform. At one point he rushed home to his nearby mansion, Friar Park, for some incense to cover the smell of fish coming from the kitchen. Typically, it wasn't fashionable at HandMade to eat meat.

But as the evening wore on and the crowd grew more raucous, Harrison's mood darkened. Perhaps the notoriously private man was shocked to realize how few of the people involved with HandMade he actually knew. Perhaps, too, he was aware that the company's financial fortunes, once so rosy, had been heading south for some time.

Whatever. When he rose to his feet, he was ready to sign the company's death warrant. "The gist of his speech was, 'Who the fuck are all you people, and where has all my money gone?'" recounts one HandMade executive. Another recalls, "He stood up and said, 'You load of freeloaders, why am I doing this?' It was appalling behavior. Rock star behavior."

O'Brien would later claim to friends that he spent the next day dissuading the company's bankers from immediately pulling the plug. At that stage, HandMade, which had lost all the money it made from early hits such as *Life of Brian* and *Time Bandits,* was kept afloat only by Harrison's financial guarantees. The banks, understandably, no longer believed Harrison was committed.

Shortly afterward, Harrison, who was only an occasional visitor to the swanky Cadogan Square office, sent an abrupt fax firing everyone—or at least everyone he knew by name. O'Brien, who was abroad on a business trip, flew home to break the news to his partner that, despite the fact that

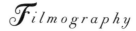

Filmography

Harrison was financing the company, he didn't actually have the power to fire anyone. A compromise was reached. Around ten staffers were made redundant, and the company staggered on.

But the spirit of fun and camaraderie that had buoyed HandMade in its early success was gone. The company produced a couple more movies, but nothing after 1990. Behind the scenes, the relationship between Harrison and O'Brien was unraveling, as the ex-Beatle began to realize how much his trust had been abused to fund his manager's imperial ambitions and lifestyle.

Not long after the fateful tenth anniversary, Cooper, a musician who was Harrison's closest friend within the company, and John Reiss, a consultant for and the managing director of O'Brien's management firm EuroAtlantic, visited Friar Park to present Harrison with evidence of O'Brien's alleged double-dealing.

Reiss says that O'Brien promptly fired him. Harrison, who hated any kind of confrontation, didn't immediately react. But, ultimately, these allegations became part of an acrimonious lawsuit that Harrison brought against O'Brien, after the company was sold in 1994.

In 1996, Harrison was awarded eleven million dollars in damages against O'Brien by the Los Angeles Superior Court, a decision upheld by a federal appeals court in California two years later. In July of 2001, however, O'Brien managed to get a court ruling protecting him from paying up, after Harrison, citing poor health, failed to show up at the hearing.

This sour ending was a far cry from the creative idealism of HandMade's early years, when Harrison's indulgence and enthusiasm helped to create one of the most distinctive brands in British cinema history. "Those first few years were a joyful period for George and Ray," says Stephen Woolley, who coproduced Neil Jordan's *Mona Lisa.* "They had success, and they had encouraged the right talent."

Woolley and Jordan first met Harrison at a lunch with Cooper a few days after they had signed the deal for *Mona Lisa.* "It was incredibly exciting to meet him," says Woolley. "He was just a charming, nice guy who benignly blessed our project. What struck you was what a gentle, kind person he was. He spoke very calmly about movies, about the things he liked.

"With *Mona Lisa,* he really liked the story, though he kind of felt there was a bit too much violence and bad language for him. He just didn't have a vicious streak in him. He told us that it wasn't the kind of movie he responded to emotionally but that he responded to Neil's talent."

Simon Relph, a producer of the early HandMade comedy *Privates on Parade,* formed a similar impression of Harrison's unintrusive patronage: "George didn't presume to intervene or give notes. He was sensibly shy of doing that. What we got from George was a great sense of commitment to the idea of asking talented people to do interesting things."

Quite simply, Harrison loved collaborating with other artists. It was an extension of his "little brother" role in

the Beatles, where he spent far more time enhancing the genius of John Lennon and Paul McCartney than on imposing his own ego.

Page 202: The budding moviemaker, circa 1964. Above: Harrison partying with Monty Python's Eric Idle and friends in 1976.

"He's a creative person, and I think he recognized other creative persons," says director David Leland, who became a close friend when he made the 1989 Jeff Daniels black comedy *Checking Out.* "He loved the whole process of hanging out and playing the music, or hanging out where the film was being made. He used to turn up to the set and say, 'Just give me something to hold, a broom or something.' In one scene he plays the janitor in an orange overall, polishing the floor."

Above all, Harrison loved hanging out with the Monty Python gang. "George is an out-and-out Python fan," says Leland. "You can see the crossover between that kind of humor and his lyrics."

HandMade was born of Harrison's Python fandom. After he appeared in Eric Idle's Beatles-spoof TV movie, *The Rutles (a.k.a. All You Need Is Cash),* the

Pythons approached him to rescue *Life of Brian.* The project's religious satire had scared off other financiers. Harrison took a leap of faith, and HandMade was created to produce the film.

The new company's next move was to pick up *The Long Good Friday* (1980), a violent drama about London gangsters, which Black Lion Films had produced but was afraid to release.

"George did rather enjoy being the savior of the British film industry," says one HandMade executive. The 1980s were dark and cautious days for British filmmaking, but HandMade rapidly won a reputation as a

beacon in the gloom. The company went on to back *Monty Python Live at the Hollywood Bowl* and several solo Python projects, including Terry Gilliam's *Time Bandits* and Michael Palin's *The Missionary.*

Probably Harrison's greatest artistic involvement was with *Time Bandits,* for which he composed the score. The film was, typically, a big gamble. "It was only Terry's second film, after *Jabberwocky,* and it wasn't easy for him to get films made," says Leland.

After failing to secure the U.S. sale he was looking for, O'Brien upped the ante even further by funding the U.S. release himself, risking $5.5 million on marketing. The film's success left HandMade awash with money. But it wasn't long before the Pythons fell out with

O'Brien and left with HandMade accountant Steve Abbott to form their own company, Prominent Features.

O'Brien's ambitions began to grow beyond Britain's cottage industry of eccentric talents. He hailed from St. Louis, and *Time Bandits* emboldened him to believe that he had a unique insight into the American market. In the mid-1980s, HandMade opened U.S. offices and started to develop American films. "Denis went a bit Hollywood," recalls one HandMade insider. "He became involved with bigger American films that weren't necessarily George's bag."

The first was the notorious turkey *Shanghai Surprise,* starring the then-married Madonna and Sean Penn. At eighteen million dollars, it was the company's most expensive film to date, and it swiftly ran into trouble on set. Harrison personally intervened as peacemaker between Penn, Madonna and director Jim Goddard. He also contributed a couple of songs. But all to no avail.

HandMade was never the same after *Shanghai Surprise.* "There did seem to be a sense that the company had lost its way," says one executive. O'Brien began recutting movies himself, against the wishes of the filmmakers. "George didn't know how bad Denis was," says Woolley. "Denis was taking on the mantle of creative decision making, because he held the purse strings."

A string of oddball flops followed. No one could accuse O'Brien of playing it safe with Harrison's money. There was *Powwow Highway,* a mystical Native American road movie; *Track 29,* a bizarre Oedipal comedy about a frustrated housewife and her long-lost son; and *Cold Dog Soup,* about one man's hapless attempts to dispose of a dead pooch in multiethnic Los Angeles, which turned out to be HandMade's final film.

And where was Harrison in all this? "He dipped in and out," says one witness. He had some personal film projects with his rock star friends that never panned out, including a film of the Traveling Wilburys that Leland was going to direct.

Many of HandMade's filmmakers had minimal dealings with Harrison, but the Wilburys film meant that Leland was more involved than most. "George had a little video camera, and we were evolving how to make a film of the album," he recounts. "I remember a great shot by George from up the stairs at an an-

gle, just of Bob Dylan's hands composing music on his piano." But the film fizzled out because of contractual problems.

Meanwhile, the losses were mounting up at HandMade. "George turned a blind eye," says an insider. "He didn't want to know if things weren't going well. So he does bear some culpability for what happened. As they lost more and more money, Denis became more and more of a control freak. But the irony is that no amount of editing would have saved most of those films."

HandMade typically financed its movies with a small amount of cash from Harrison and often from his friends, such as Elton John, as well as a large amount in bank loans. These were partly secured on distribution deals and partly on Harrison's name.

Harrison believed that O'Brien shared joint responsibility for the loan guarantees. But, in truth, his was the only name on the contracts. At one stage in the late 1980s, when a bank asked to see a personal balance sheet for Harrison, it revealed that the ex-Beatle's potential liabilities outweighed his assets to the tune of thirty-two million dollars.

HandMade had brought Harrison to the brink of bankruptcy. But most of the company's staff and filmmakers suspected nothing.

"It was a good time, until I realized what was going on," says John Reiss. "O'Brien ran the place with a rod of iron. People weren't on great money but stayed as much out of loyalty to George as anything."

Which was why Harrison's eruption at the tenth-birthday bash came as such a shock. "He's not an aggressive, confrontational guy," says Woolley, who had fallen out with O'Brien so badly that he wasn't even invited to the party, even though *Mona Lisa* was one of the company's biggest hits. "George is a sweetheart. And that was the problem."

Even then, it took Harrison several more years to extricate himself from O'Brien's web. In the end, the CD revolution came along to rescue his personal finances. He never returned to filmmaking. But when the bitterness is long forgotten, the films will remain as a testament to the courage of Harrison's creative beliefs.

As Leland says, "He didn't need to be making films, he just wanted to make films with certain types of people. It was very much a personal thing." ✳

By Andy Babiuk

STRINGS OF {HIS HEART

WHEN THE BEATLES' MANAGER, Brian Epstein, secured a recording contract with EMI in 1962, he sent a telegram to the band in Hamburg, Germany: "Congratulations boys. EMI request recording session. Please rehearse new material." The Beatles replied to the telegram with postcards. Paul McCartney wrote, "Please wire £10,000 advance royalties." John Lennon scribbled, "When are we going to be millionaires?" But George Harrison made the following request: "Please order four new guitars." While his band mates visualized piles of money, Harrison could think only about guitars.

Most young guitarists dream about and lust after seemingly unobtainable instruments, and Harrison was no exception. The teenage Harrison daydreamed about guitars, drawing pictures of them in his schoolbooks and studying record covers of his heroes, longing for such instruments as the Fender Stratocaster. If he'd had his way, he recalled later, the Strat would have been his first guitar. He had seen Buddy Holly's Strat on the *"Chirping" Crickets* album cover and tried to find one. But in Liverpool in those days, the only thing he came upon resembling a Strat was a Futurama. It was difficult to play, the strings about half an inch off the fingerboard–but it did look sort of futuristic.

In 1960, the Beatles were playing in Hamburg, and seventeen-year-old Harrison wrote home to a Liverpool friend, Arthur Kelly. The letter was packed with information indicating just how much Harrison thought about guitars. He wrote about another British musician who was playing in Hamburg at the time, Tony Sheridan, saying, "He's now got a Fender guitar and amp like [Buddy Holly's], and I play it well. It also has a vibrato and his bass player has a Fender bass." Harrison continued, "Look out as I am thinking of getting yet again another new guitar. I may leave solids out of it this time and get an Everly Brother–type massive Gibson as they are gear." Then he gave Kelly some vital information needed to send off for a free Fender catalogue, carefully writing out the company's address in Santa Ana, California. "I might manage a red Fender Stratocaster with gold plating," Harrison wrote–but added that the guitar he really wanted was made by Gretsch.

"When I was in Hamburg, I found out that some guy had a Stratocaster for sale," Harrison later recalled in Ray Minhinnett and Bob Young's *The Story of the Fender Stratocaster.* "I arranged that I was going to go first thing the next morning and buy it. I believe it was a white one. And this fellow who was the guitar player in Rory Storm and the Hurricanes . . . found out about it, too, and he got up earlier and went and bought it. By the time I got there it had gone. I was so disappointed it scarred me for life, that experience. I think after that happened I got the Gretsch–it was a denial kind of thing." Johnny Guitar, lead guitarist in Rory Storm and the Hurricanes, said that the incident led to a fistfight over the guitar: "I asked Rory why he was lending the Beatles the money when our own guitarist, Ty Brian, needed one [a guitar]. When we got there, Rory told them he'd changed his mind and we were buying the guitar for Ty. All hell broke loose and Lennon went mad, but Ty held his own, rolling around the floor. They ignored us for a few days after, but it all blew over."

Back home, Harrison bought his first Gretsch. "I saw an ad in the pa-

per in Liverpool," he told *Guitar Player,* "and there was a guy selling his guitar. I bought [a Gretsch Duo Jet from a sailor] who had bought it in America and brought it back. It was my first real American guitar–and I'll tell you, it was secondhand, but I polished that thing. I was so proud to own that." This was the start of Harrison's love affair with Gretsch guitars. He would later add to his collection the guitars he is most associated with, the Gretsch Chet Atkins Country Gentleman and Tennessean models.

Guitarist Colin Manley of the Remo Four remembers how he and Harrison would talk guitars at school. The pair discovered Chet Atkins together at a Duane Eddy concert, where Eddy played "Trambone" and announced that it was an Atkins song. Keen to discover more about this new name, the two got hold of an Atkins LP featuring "Trambone," with its multiple picked parts. "Well," Manley says in astonishment, "that was it! It was like, 'How does he do that?' So we found out about Chet and just took it from there. We liked some different guitar players, but we both loved Chet. George came around to my house a couple of times, and we'd listen to Chet and try to work out how he did it."

As the Beatles' popularity grew, so did Harrison's guitar collection. From early on, Lennon and Harrison liked the idea of matching guitars, each acquiring a Gibson J-160E electric-acoustic. Later, while visiting his sister in the United States in 1963, Harrison purchased a Rickenbacker 425 electric guitar and had it painted black to match Lennon's little Rickenbacker 325.

Opposite: Restringing the Rickenbacker, with his Gretsch Country Gentleman alongside. Above: Playing his Rickenbacker backstage on the Beatles' first North American tour, in 1964.

In February 1964, during the Beatles' first U.S. visit to perform on *The Ed Sullivan Show*, Rickenbacker gave Harrison its new twelve-string electric guitar. He immediately took it back to England and used it on many of the songs that would appear in the group's film *A Hard Day's Night*.

Roger McGuinn of the Byrds credits Harrison for his own use of a Rickenbacker twelve-string. McGuinn recalls that as the Byrds got together they made a couple of trips to see *A Hard Day's Night*, taking note of the Beatles' instruments. "George had this guitar that looked like a six-string from the front," says McGuinn. "But when he turned sideways you could see six more pegs sticking out the back. I said, 'Ah, that's an electric twelve, that's really cool.' So I went out and bought one." McGuinn says the Byrds' sound was directly shaped by Harrison's use of the Rickenbacker twelve-string. The Byrds, in turn, influenced countless other bands who would put the Rick 12 at the center of their own sound. Directly and indirectly, Harrison's choice of guitar changed the musical landscape of the 1960s.

Harrison's taste in instruments continued to grow. His use of a sitar on "Norwegian Wood" was unprecedented. "It was George Harrison who introduced Indian music to the Western culture," Ravi

I saw a guitar program on TV, and it got into how guitars are phallic and sexual. Maybe that's so. I don't know in my case, but ever since I was a kid I've loved guitars and songs about them.

—GEORGE HARRISON

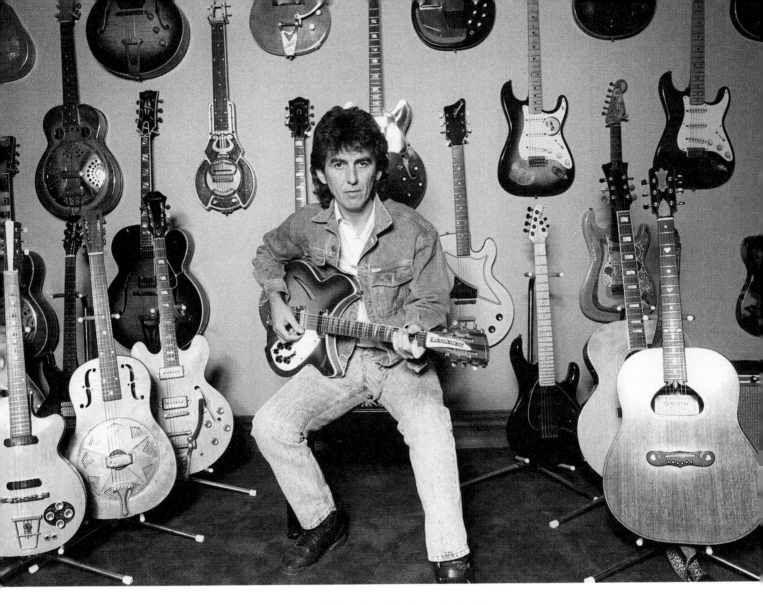

Shankar emphasized to me. Many bands followed suit with recordings featuring Indian instruments. Harrison again effectively changed the sound of the times.

Going back to his first love, Harrison finally got a Fender Strat, which he painted in psychedelic colors and affectionately named Rocky. And Fender later made Harrison a special Telecaster out of rosewood, which he used in the film *Let It Be*. In December 1969, Harrison joined Delaney and Bonnie's backing band, billed as Eric Clapton and Friends. After the first night, Harrison presented Delaney Bramlett with a generous gift: his Fender Rosewood Telecaster. Handing over the guitar, he told Bramlett that it was "for what you did for me last night."

Giving or receiving an instrument as a gift seemed almost sacred to Harrison, and he frequently gave away guitars to his close friends as a token of friendship. In the same way, Harrison held in high esteem a gift from Clapton: a Gibson Les Paul named Lucy, the same guitar that Clapton used to play the lead on "While My Guitar Gently Weeps." It was far more than just another guitar to Harrison, so he was particularly shocked when, in the early 1970s, his beloved Les Paul was stolen. "It got kidnapped and taken to Guadalajara," he said later. "I had to buy this Mexican guy a Les Paul to get it back." But it was worth it—all for the love of a guitar. ✳

With his collection, 1987: "When I was thirteen," he said, "I would sit at the back of class and draw guitars. I even tried making a guitar."

THE *Best* OF HARRISON *Collectibles*

WALLPAPER. Pomade. School bags. Kazoos. In the mid-Sixties, the Beatles' name was plastered on an absurd variety of products. Today, collectors fork over equally absurd sums of money for memorabilia that once could be bought with a child's weekly allowance. Following his death, George Harrison–related collectibles were expected to increase in value by at least 50 percent. (Autographed copies of his 1979 limited-edition autobiography, *I Me Mine,* were being sold on online auction sites for two thousand dollars.)

"[Beatles manager] Brian Epstein had no idea what kind of demand there would be for Beatles stuff," says Danny Bennett, who began building his collection as a ten-year-old during the band's heyday. Epstein established merchandising agreements allowing manufactur-

ers and middlemen to keep 90 percent of the profits. The Beatles and Epstein split the rest. "It's ridiculous," says Bennett, who manages musicians, including his father, Tony. "These days, it would be the opposite."

Bennett owns four hundred items, but he says his hobby has never been about money. "True collectors don't collect to invest," he explains. "I saved these things because they meant something to me." His most prized collectibles come from the 1966 Shea Stadium concert in New York. The promoter brought Danny and his brother backstage to meet the Beatles. When they were left alone in the dressing room, Danny's budding collector instinct kicked in: "The airline tags were still on their instrument cases. So I clipped them and kept them. Years later I had Paul McCartney sign them for me." ❋

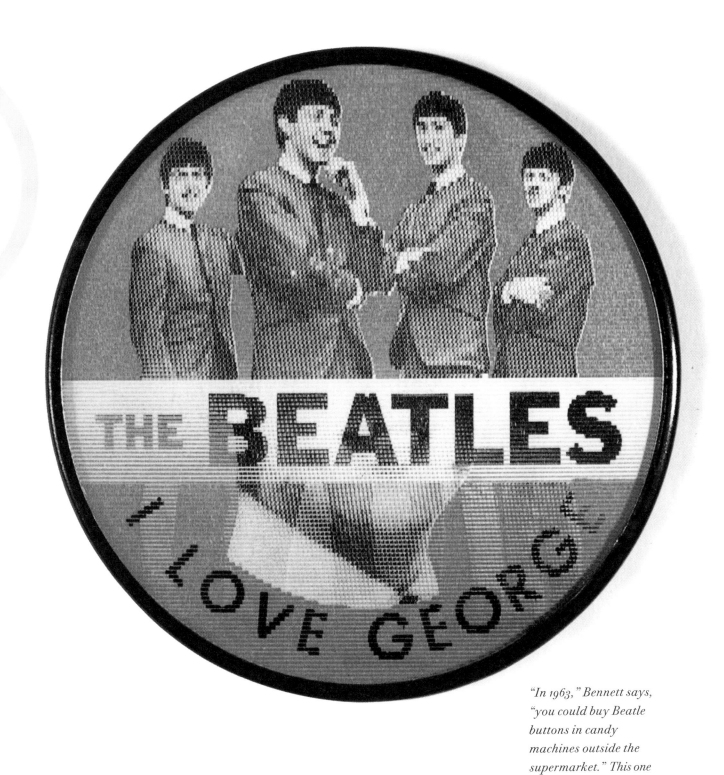

"In 1963," Bennett says, *"you could buy Beatle buttons in candy machines outside the supermarket." This one is worth ten dollars.*

Opposite page, clockwise from top: The earliest Beatle dolls, circa 1964; Beatles jigsaw puzzle; a popular 1966 do-it-yourself model kit; a recently produced ceramic "Something" container that Bennett received as a gift; an inflatable Harrison, available in 1967 from Lux soap. This page: A mid-Sixties Harrison doll, produced in 1991.

George Harrison

217

THE FABULOUS
BEATLES
JEWELRY BROOCH

MANUFACTURED IN U.S.A. 1000
COPYRIGHT 1964 REGD. DESIGN
By arrangement with The "BEATLES"
NEMS ENTERPRISES, LTD.

SID BERNSTEIN, Presents

NO REFUNDS — NO EXCHANGES

SHEA STADIUM
ENTER GATE D
FIELD LEVEL BOX $5.75
109K
BOX
TUE, AUG. 23, 1966-7:30 P.M.
3
SEAT

WOW!
the Beatles
ARE HERE!
the only
AUTHENTIC
BEATLE WIG

MB
KEY
TO FUN

THE **BEATLES**

FOR
AGES
7 to 15

MILTON
BRADLEY
COMPANY
SPRINGFIELD
MASSACHUSETTS
4404
MADE IN USA

FLIP YOUR WIG GAME

Opposite page, clockwise from top left: Beatle brooch; Bennett's ticket to the 1966 Shea Stadium concert; the Flip Your Wig board game; a lunchbox set that is now worth a thousand dollars; "Everyone bought Beatles wigs," Bennett says, "because nobody had long hair." This page: Only five thousand of these phonographs were made in 1964. Original price, thirty dollars—today, a mint one goes for eight thousand dollars.

BOB DYLAN

KEITH RICHARDS

TOM PETTY

MICK JAGGER

YOKO ONO

ELTON JOHN

PAUL SIMON

JIM KELTNER

Interviews by

✳ ✳ ✳

MIM UDOVITCH
and DAVID WILD

BOB DYLAN

HE WAS A GIANT, a great, great soul, with all the humanity, all the wit and humor, all the wisdom, the spirituality, the common sense of a man and compassion for people. He inspired love and had the strength of a hundred men. He was like the sun, the flowers and the moon, and we will miss him enormously. The world is a profoundly emptier place without him. ✽

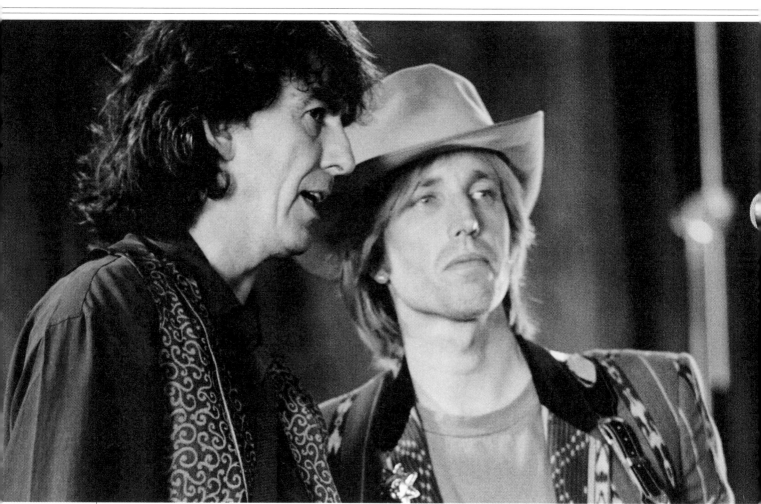

66 *I'm blessed* 99

TO HAVE KNOWN HIM.

TOM PETTY

FIRST MET HIM

in 1974 when I came out to Los Angeles. I hadn't been out here very long. I was working at Leon Russell's, and there were a few nights with sessions with George and Ringo. It's a scary thing meeting Beatles, but George was so nice to me and included me in everything. Then our paths didn't cross again until years later; this was probably '85 or '86, when the Heartbreakers were touring England with Bob Dylan. George came one night to see us in Birmingham. Bob was busy with something and so we wound up just talking.

I reminded him that we'd met, and there was some kind of weird click. It felt like we had known each other all our lives—and in a very personal way. We wound up just hanging a lot. I have a great photo somewhere—it was my birthday, and George brought a little cake to my dressing room. In the photo, there is me with George and Jeff Lynne, Roger McGuinn, Bob Dylan and Mike Campbell—all of my favorite people right there, and it was so sweet. That night there was a surprise hurricane in London, and my life never felt the same again after that hurricane.

"He taught me so much": Harrison and Petty as Wilburys in 1988.

I went back to L.A., and almost by fate I went into a restaurant, spur of the moment. I hadn't planned to go, and the waiter came over and said, "Your friend is in the next room, he wants to see you." I didn't know who he meant. I walked in, and it was George. He said, "It's so weird, I was just asking Jeff Lynne for your number." He said, "Where are you going?" I said, "I'm just going home." He said, "Do you mind if I go with you?" He came to my house and stayed for days.

George came to L.A. fairly often, and I went to England and visited him a lot. That's going to be the hard thing—going to England from now on. It will seem so strange with him not there. See, George really treasured his friends. Mike Campbell was saying, "George was the only kind of friend I knew who would bring you a gift every time he saw you." He once brought me four ukuleles in a week. I said, "George, I don't think I need four ukuleles." He said, "Well, this one is better than the other ones. And it's just good to have them here–you never know when we're going to need them."

George's idea of a band was that everybody hung. From what he told me, the Beatles were that way. They were very, very tight. He wanted the Traveling Wilburys to be like that. Like, "If we're going to the party, we're all going." I'm so glad I got to be in a band with him. He taught me so much.

What was it like being in a band with Bob Dylan?

George quoted Bob like people quote Scripture. Bob really adored George, too. George used to hang over the balcony videoing Bob while Bob wasn't aware of it. Bob would be sitting at the piano playing, and George would tape it and listen to it all night.

So George had his own private Dylan bootlegs?

Yeah. One day George was hiding in the hedge at the house where we were recording. As everybody flew off, George would rise up out of the bushes with his video going. And he did that with Bob. I think George frightened Bob. When the Wilburys started, George was so reverent of Bob. At the end of the first day, he said, "We know that you're Bob Dylan and everything, but we're going to just treat you and talk to you like we would anybody else." And Bob went, "Well, great. Believe it or not, I'm in awe of you guys, and it's the same for me." I said to George, "That is really amazing, how you said that to Bob." George goes, "I can say those sort of things. But you can't" [*laughs*]. George adored Bob Dylan, like, "Dylan makes Shakespeare look like Billy Joel." And George absolutely adored the Wilburys. That was his baby from the beginning, and he went at it with such great enthusiasm. The rest of his life, he considered himself a Wilbury.

It doesn't really sound like he was the quiet one.

Well, he never shut up. George had a lot to say. Boy, did he have a lot to say. That's hysterical to me, you know, that he was known as the quiet one. I assume he got that name because the other ones were so much louder. I mean, they were very loud people [*laughs*]. One time he told me, "Me and Olivia had Paul and Linda over the other night, and you would have thought there was a hundred people in the house, it was so loud." I'll tell you, nobody I've encountered ever lived his life more every day than George did. And he had an idea a minute. Some nights he would have so many great ideas. George really said everything that crossed his mind. And he was painfully honest. It was an endearing trait, but sometimes you hoped that he wouldn't be quite as honest as he was going to be.

Was it sometimes difficult to be around him?

Let's be honest. There was Cranky George, and he could be very cynical at times. He would always be the first to nail himself as being too cynical, but he was quite funny when he was really cynical.

How did he feel about the Beatles as he got older?

I just know what I've heard from George as the years went by. But he was very funny, like, "The Beatles, they weren't all that they were cracked up to be" [*laughs*]. He loved the Beatles. He used to bitch sometimes about individual Beatles who got on his nerves. But he really loved them down deep, and I knew this. I think that a lot of George's personality was formed by John. This is just a guess, but that was the way it appeared to me. He looked up to John so much. He said, "Oh, John would be a Wilbury in a second." He'd say about Paul, "Paul is a year older than me, and he still is." But he really loved Paul, too. And he really loved Ringo.

What George Harrison songs mean the most to you?

There are so many. "Here Comes the Sun" always has a big effect on me. "Isn't It a Pity" is a masterpiece.

Any of the songs you recorded with him?

I loved "End of the Line." I remember the day he wrote it. He had started it off on the piano. And we all kind of sat in a group. His enthusiasm was very contagious. One of the things I'll miss most is when he used to drop by and he would have a guitar or a ukulele in his hands most of the evening. He taught me so much guitar. I miss him showing me the guitar and some Beatles lick that I never could figure out. He would show me these licks, and they would be the simplest things in the world, but they'd eluded me because I didn't think they could be that simple. But what a beautiful player he was. He had that extreme taste. He was something on the guitar.

And the ukulele, too?

It sounds corny, but the ukulele gave him so much joy. He played the hell out of the thing. When my kids were little, we cleared rooms with those things, because they knew George was going to carry on till daylight.

For a guy who loved music and people so much, he rarely played in public.

He was never far from music. The last time he came over here, which wasn't that long ago, he was playing the guitar and singing me new songs that he had written, which were just so beautiful. I said, "I wish you would just put a mike up, and let's tape you just like this." He didn't want to do it–"Maybe later." But he told me something once like, "I never really pursued a solo career. *All Things Must Pass* was a reaction to leaving the Beatles." When that went so well, he made another one. But he never had a manager or anybody to report to, and I don't think he had any interest in touring. He told me many times he was uncomfortable being the guy up front having to sing all the songs.

The thing he was proudest of was the Beatles. He said the Beatles put out such a positive message. I remember him visiting me on tour in Germany. He would come to the side of the stage and look out. But he really didn't want to go on. He would go, "It's so loud and smoky, and they are acting so crazy. I just feel better back here."

I was listening to a song you two wrote together, "Cheer Down." Where did that one come from?

Olivia would say that to George when he got a little too happy. He would get a burst of enthusiasm, and she'd say, "Okay, cheer down, big fellow."

Were you impressed with Olivia's defense of George when he was attacked in their home in 1999?

When I heard about it, I sent George a fax, and it just said, "Aren't you glad you married a Mexican girl?" [*Laughs*] Olivia really kicked ass. She is a beautiful person. His son, Dhani, is a beautiful kid, man. I've seen him recently. He is doing very well–very strong and inspired. Olivia had the hardest job in the world, because she loved George more than all of us, and she really took care of him and cleared the path in front of him, behind him, and inherited that crazy life, you know.

Do you believe his spiritual life helped him cope with what had to be a horrible few years?

I would think it helped him immensely. He is just a really brave guy, and he died with a great deal of dignity. It's so much easier for me than if he had died that night in the attack. I don't think I could have dealt with that. I told him so. When I put on my TV the morning he was

stabbed, it looked like he had died, there were so many biographical things coming up on the TV. After that, I told him, "I already kind of went through your death." And I said, "Just do me a favor and don't die that way, because I just can't handle it." He said he promised me he wasn't going out that way.

Not that long ago, he released a statement telling people not to worry about him. Was that characteristic?

I'll tell you, the media wasn't very sweet in the last year of his life. Especially in Europe, he never got a moment's peace. He would have helicopters follow him when he left the house. I guess that's part of the price you pay. But he'd be the first to say there's nothing to be gained by bitterness or anger, hatred. I don't know how many times he would remind me that bitterness or pessimism is only going to slow you down finding the solution. And he lived that way. George was the kind of guy who wasn't going to leave until he hugged you for five minutes and told you how much he loved you. We knew where we stood with each other.

This relationship was very important to you.

It's the only time in my life, really, that I had been that close to somebody–outside of, like, my mom dying or something. I loved him so much, and if he had never played a note, I would have been so blessed to have him in my life. It really comes home to you that, oh, wow, the whole world feels this way. They all knew him in their way, and they are mourning him as well. It was very hard, because there's a duality to it. I mourn for my friend, and then I also am a huge fan just like everyone else. I'm just blessed by God to have known him. He had so much love in him. I realized it more with him gone, that he was just pure love. My daughter Adria used to visit him a lot in England when she was over there. She would stay at Friar Park. She was telling me the other night that one night they were out walking in the garden and he goes, "Oh, Adria, sometimes I just wish I could turn into a light beam and go away."

Perhaps that's how it works.

Yeah, maybe that is how it works.

Is there anything else you'd like George Harrison fans to understand about the man you knew so well?

I would assure all his fans that George was just really as beautiful as they pictured him. And maybe more. ✻

When he was the
YOUNG MAN ABOUT TOWN,

WE USED TO BE DRINKING BUDDIES.

MICK JAGGER

Georg DESERVES RECOGNITION.
He was always rather overshadowed—there's no other way of putting it—
by John and Paul. I mean, to call him "the quiet Beatle," it's like some
dopey publicist made that up in 1964. And, of course, he was quite a
complicated person. When you say, "Oh, the quiet Beatle," it's like,

"Oh, yeah, okay, he sits in the corner." And he wasn't really that. He was very complex, and he was very charming and friendly. I notice that Bob Geldof called him curmudgeonly, which is true, you know, but people are always saying to me—and I don't want to really compare myself to George—but they say, "Gosh, you've got lots of faces." And I say, "Well, yeah, people are complex."

So George was very friendly, but he also could be quite quarrelsome at times. He had a side of him which, if he felt you deserved it, so to speak, would lash out at you. But I'm talking about when he was much, much younger; I never saw that side of him later on in life. But when he was the young man around town, I used to see him a lot. We used to see each other in nightclubs and so on and be drinking buddies. I suppose what I'm trying to say is, he wasn't just a retiring person only, in my mind. He could be funny and charming and also quite acerbic. He had the sort of quality that normally people would associate with John.

And then, later, George developed this other side to him. He very much concentrated on the spiritual side of his life, and it was more than a passing fancy. It looked like it was a sort of faddish thing at the time, but it stayed with him. You got the feeling that most people were dabbling in spirituality, but for George it was perhaps the major part of his life once he discovered it. And it's very easy to ridicule someone who does that, and he was ridiculed, there's no doubt about that, especially in England, for being like that. But he did follow through on the courage of his convictions. He stayed with it and never rejected it. And, of course, he made mistakes—anybody following this who was one of the first people of a generation to do that would make mistakes—but not any glaring ones. You've got to start somewhere.

Another thing he did that was groundbreaking was, of course, the idea of rock & roll linked with charity, which was a generous thing and was also linked to his generosity of spirit and his spirituality. It was a very innovative thing, even with all the problems that it had. And "While My Guitar Gently Weeps"? It's lovely,

plaintive. Only a guitar player could write that; I love that song. And "My Sweet Lord": There's tons of songs with that chord sequence, but that's a very nice one. As a guitar player, he certainly had some nice and memorable licks on those Beatles tunes. Without being a virtuoso, he came up with really nice guitar lines that are integral parts of those tunes. But he wasn't just a guitar player. And he did have a sense of humor, and he did take it all with a huge pinch of salt, which is a very English and a very Liverpudlian thing.

I hadn't seen George for a very long time. He came to a concert that the Stones did in a theater in London called the Brixton Academy, in July 1995. And he said to Charlie [*in Liverpool accent*], "You're very lucky to be in a working band." And it was really nice to see him. He went through periods of be-

With Jagger at the Rock & Roll Hall of Fame ceremony in 1988

ing reclusive, and it was lovely to see him. We would see each other rarely after the Sixties and middle Seventies.

Really, whatever I say about my feelings is ridiculous and inadequate. It's very difficult to depersonalize it. It's like part of your life. But, you know, that's probably what most people think. Because the Beatles were a big part of one's life. And when someone like that dies, in a way, a part of your own life is gone.   ❋

KEITH RICHARDS

I REMEMBER THE FIRST TIME I met George, we were doing our usual bar gig in West London. Suddenly these four guys in black leather overcoats were standing in the doorway, and then I get a sort of elbow in the ribs from Mick or Brian: "It's the Beatles!" So the first time I set eyes on George, or any of them, was that vision like, *"They look just like their record cover!"* At the time we were working for fifty cents, you know?

George and I kind of formed–without talking too much about it, although we did have a laugh here and there–a bond, in that we felt we were kind of fulfilling the same role within our respective bands. It was a nod and a wink to say, "Well, they'd be nowhere without us." He was a very quiet and enigmatic guy in many ways. He had a very sly sense of humor, very quiet. But there was always this unspoken bond between us.

And he was really a lovely guy. What he didn't need, and to me what's unbelievable, is that, basically, the knifing–the attack two years ago at his house–is what did in George. Because I think he probably would have beaten the cancer if it wasn't for the blade. John was my first mate among them, because George was a bit quiet.

we felt we **FULFILLED THE SAME ROLE** *within our bands.*

Now I think, "Oh, one by gun, one by knife." And that's still puzzling to me in a way, although he didn't die literally from it. It's just that for such pleasant guys, who made such beautiful music and never did harm to anybody, to have to go through that kind of violence—I mean, I'm used to it, I've been stabbed several times, and the bullet wounds are healing.

George didn't write that many songs, but the ones he did write were very meaningful, very well worked out—he was an incredibly meticulous man with respect to his work and to what he wanted to do. The record speaks for itself—"[While My] Guitar Gently Weeps," "Something," "My Sweet Lord." When he put something out, he worked on it a long time and got it right the way he wanted it, which is a very difficult thing to do.

He could be a very funny guy when he wanted to be. And I sort of remember those times more than the last few years—like the time the cops waited until he left my house to move in for the drug bust in 1969. George always used to rub that in, you know: "Well, that's the difference between the Beatles and the Stones: The Stones get busted when the Beatles leave." Unfortunately, they got busted soon after, but that was more harassment than anything.

I think the other thing that runs between George and the Beatles and ourselves, the Stones, is that we're basically the same age and happened to find ourselves in this unique position without any training. You know what I mean? You can't go to star school. And George was never interested in that. George reminds me very much of Charlie Watts, in that way and in many ways—the understatedness, the modesty and just being a gentleman, really. There's very few I'd give that word to, and I wouldn't give it to myself. But he was a gent.

The last time I saw him was when he came to a Stones gig in London, and he came disguised as Farmer George. He was a great horticulturalist. George loved his garden, another sign of a real gent. He came backstage, and he was full of beans then. I just said, "How are you doing, healing and shit?" And he said, "Okay," you know. He seemed all right. I'm quite happy that I last saw him when he was on an up.

His spiritual trip is another thing, but I don't want to go into it because I don't know anything about it. As I always said to George, I draw the line at swamis. You know? I always treated it as an interesting thing, like, well, why not learn a bit more about esoteric Eastern religions? But I don't know anything about all this Ganges stuff. One river's very much like another, they all flow into the same sea.

What I know is that he was a lovely lead guitarist, beautifully understated. The thing is, you've got your Jimi Hendrix, you've got your Eric Clapton, and then you've got guys who can play with bands. And George was a band and a team player. People get carried away with lead guitars, and *blu-du-blu-du-blu-du-blu,* and feedbacks. And it's all histrionics, when it comes down to it. George was an artist, but he was also a fucking craftsman. When you listen to his songs, you're aware of how much went into it. He didn't flip anything off. George crafted his stuff very, very carefully, and it all had its own feel.

This was a guy who could come out with a great song or a great record anytime. I was always waiting for some more. Let's hope there's more in the can. I always loved "Guitar Gently Weeps," because that was a guitar-player thing. And "Here Comes the Sun"—it's just beauty. Beauty. What can you say? Still waters run deep. I have no doubt that there was a whole lot inside of George, and a whole lot he never revealed. But at the same time, every time he did something, he did reveal a little bit of himself. So that in fact you think you know George better than George knew himself.

I'm going to miss him. And if there is anything like heaven and shit like that, hopefully John and him are saying, "How you doing, pal, want a drink?" You just have to wish him well. I just hope he's jamming with John. The spirit lives. The thing is, you make a record or two, and there's a little bit of immortality there. George left his mark, man. I don't think I can say anything else except, "George: Miss you. Bless you. And we're still listening to you."   ✳

" HE *was a* MAN *of*

wit and humor.

"

by

✳ ✳ ✳ ✳ ✳ YOKO ONO ✳ ✳ ✳ ✳ ✳

JOHN LOVED GEORGE, and George loved John. Their friendship was a very special one. John was always concerned about George's songs not getting just treatment. It's a famous story how John insisted on breaking the tradition and making "Something" the first original Beatles single that was not Lennon-McCartney. George remembered. Since John's passing, George, Olivia and Dhani sent Sean and I beautiful exotic flowers of Hawaii every Christmas.

George was so many things to the world: He was an innovative guitar player, a songwriter with words of wisdom and a man who introduced Eastern philosophy and music to the West. But in his private life, he was a man of wit and humor who made his friends laugh.

George had a green thumb, too. He made things grow, like what they say Indian music does. Well, George did it, and in style. He single-handedly created a huge and beautiful garden in his estate, which he designed and tended to daily. I'll never forget how proudly he took me around the garden one day, in his muddy rubber boots and an old hoe in his hand, checking each tree and flower as if they were his children and, at the same time, caring for the steps I took. That's the George I will always remember: a man in his garden smiling warmly to me like some Indian guru.

I received a call at three o'clock in the morning from Olivia. I immediately knew what it was about. It reminded me of the calls I made when John passed away. It also reminded me of the sense of propriety and responsibility all of us Beatle women quietly shared. Olivia is an intelligent and strong woman. But that doesn't mean that she can take an enormous parting such as this. There are things you can never take, no matter how strong you are. I hope the world will be kind to her and Dhani. At twenty-three, Dhani is already a highly intelligent and strong member of the Harrisons and the family of the Beatles—a family of a rock band, which once lost John and now George. ✳

“the GUY had a WAY of HANDLING EVERYTHING so beautifully.”

JIM KELTNER

IT JUST HURTS so bad to know that he's not going to be coming around anymore and calling. I want to hear that beautiful, soft accent. Forget his singing, I mean, I used to just love to just listen to him talk. And all the funny stories about him recently about being "the quiet Beatle"–he was the most talkative person I know. But the beautiful thing about George was that he always had something to say. I used to see people get their feelings hurt being around him. It was almost as if he couldn't not tell the truth.

What brought you two together?

George always loved Ry Cooder. Ry was a huge influence on him. It was the musical connection, I think, because he used to always talk about Ry and his music. He was also Bob Dylan's biggest fan. He could quote the lyrics to practically any Dylan song that you came up with. So I think that was a good, solid connection between the two of us–my association with Bob and Ry. And then, of course, when I started playing with John Lennon, that went a long way, too–because to describe George's relationship with John is to say that John was truly his big brother. George was very, very heavily influenced by John, all of John's thinking and the way John did things in the world, and the way he handled his Beatledom, you know. I can't ever describe properly what it's like to have been so close with all those guys. With George there was a closeness, like, really, truly a brother. I mean, that's such a cliché.

Was it meaningful for you to have spent some time with him at the end of his life?

Oh, God, you can't imagine. My whole deal with George was that I never gave up for a minute, not even till the very last second. We saw him on Sunday, and he died on Thursday, and I didn't believe it. When we left him that day, we were walking three feet off the ground as we got to the car. We had been talking and laughing with him a little bit, and he seemed to have rallied and had his strength, and it was just so wonderful. God, it was just fantastic: "Hi, Jimmy." It just was such a great gift. That's what I'm holding onto.

He seemed to die as he lived–with great dignity.

The guy just had a way of handling everything so beautifully. He was deep with his religion, and I believe that God must be blessing him immensely right now. He never changed, he never wavered. He was always talking about how great one of these days it's going to be to get out of these old bodies.

"Forget his singing, I just loved to listen to him talk."

To me he was just George. He was just George, my beautiful, beautiful friend. When he passed on, I was shocked to see the whole world eulogizing him over and over. I never thought of him as this icon. He wasn't any of those things. John and George were both like that. Here I come into their lives, and I'm going, "Oh, man, hey, what was this like?" and "What was that like?" Beatle this, Beatle that, and they wouldn't have it, you know. They finally instilled upon me that, hey, Jimmy, you know, we're not Beatles anymore. They were trying to break that, bust that in two, so that they could move on and do something else.

"

HE
WAS
THE
Sage
OF
THE
BEATLES.
HE
FOUND
SOME-
THING
WORTH
MORE
THAN
FAME.

"

I ACTUALLY HADN'T SEEN GEORGE since Linda McCartney's memorial service. But during the older days—when I was behaving myself not too well but having basically a very good time—I have very fond memories of playing on *Cloud Nine,* George's album. And George was always very, very kind to me. When I first came to America and the *Elton John* album was, like, Number Eighteen or Nineteen on the charts, and I was pinching myself, looking at all the records on the charts by my heroes, I got a telegram from George congratulating me. I've still got it somewhere. It was just a very thoughtful thing for him to do. It meant the whole world to me.

Then, after I got to meet him and hang out with him and play on his records, he continued to be very, very generous in spirit to me. I still remember staying up until eight o'clock in the morning recording and then asking him to play "Here Comes the Sun." And he did, and it was magical.

✳ ✳ ✳ ELTON JOHN

He was very forthright, and he actually administered quite a few tellings-off to me about my drug problem. There was this one night in Los Angeles when he said, "Listen, for God's sake, go easy on the marching powder, because it's not going to do you any good." That was the evening I tried to change Bob Dylan's wardrobe. I was saying, "You can't keep going round in clothes like that, you've got to come upstairs, I'll give you a few clothes." And the look of horror on Dylan's face was unbelievable. Because, can you imagine? I was like, "Oh, yeah, I've got a couple of Versace numbers upstairs that'll really suit you, Bob." George was present for this. So he administered a little talk to me.

George always spoke his mind. He could be a little intimidating when he wasn't in a good mood, like we all can. The last time I saw him, he was a bit grumpy toward me, and I felt, "*Oooh.*" But who knows what he was having to deal with? He had a pretty rough ride the last four or five years. He didn't like celebrity. I think he'd had enough by 1970 to last three lifetimes. George just relished his gardening and his motor racing, and he loved his privacy. As a result of that reclusiveness, there was a little bit of curmudgeonly commentary about bands–saying he hated Oasis and U2 . . . bands today aren't as good. And they probably aren't. He was very forthright. There was no holding back. You know, at a time when Oasis were kissing the Beatles' feet, George Harrison said, "Well, they're rubbish."

He was a bit like an earth mother, in a way. He loved his gardening, he loved his wife, he loved his kid, he loved his house, Friar Park, and he restored that house as much as he could. I mean, it's a huge fucking house.

I think he was the kind of sage of the Beatles. He was the youngest member. But as people said, he was very spiritual and very serious about his religious beliefs. It wasn't just a five-minute-wonder thing with him. He found something worth more than fame, more than fortune, more than anything. I think that helped him the last few months of his life. Because he was pretty stoic.

As a guitarist–well, the trademark of a great guitarist is that you can always identify their sound, and with George you can always tell it's George Harrison playing. All his solos are very melodic–you can almost sing his solos. And he was his own songwriter, as well. I think *All Things Must Pass,* apart from [John Lennon's] *Walls and Bridges,* is the best post-Beatles solo album. And it shocked a lot of people, because it's such a colossal, great-sounding album, full of great songs, and it was a triple album. I don't think people expected that to come out of George Harrison. It was totally different from anything the Beatles had ever done. And I think that's a huge achievement.

I remember hearing "My Sweet Lord" in a taxi somewhere, I can't remember what city, and I thought, "Oh, my God," and I got chills. You know when a record starts on the radio, and it's great, and you think, "Oh, what is this, what is this, what is this?" The only other record I ever felt that way about was "Brown Sugar," by the Rolling Stones. "My Sweet Lord" was a song that everybody sang, and whether they thought about it consciously or not, it made another train of thought spiritually available.

Of all his songs–and I know this is such an obvious choice–I think "Something" is probably one of the best love songs ever, ever, *ever* written, and probably the best Beatles love song. It's better than "Yesterday," much better. It's a beautiful, beautiful song, structure-wise and in every way. It's like the song I've been chasing for the last thirty-five years. Every time I hear that song . . . I don't know, it just comes from where George was. It's *the* perfect song. Just one of the best songs ever written.

Basically, George was very much a man of peace. Even when he was being attacked in his house, he

*"He was like an earth mother":
Elton John with Harrison.*

wasn't fighting the guy off, he was trying to restrain him by words. So the last few years, with the throat cancer and the attack and then various business stuff going wrong, George had a lot on his plate, and he came through it a man of peace. And that says a lot for Olivia, his wife, as well.

When I think of him, I don't remember any specific conversation or anecdote. I just remember that when we hung out, music was played, conversation was provocative, and there was a lot of laughter. I feel very privileged to have known him, to have played on his records. I've played on a Lennon record. I've played on a Ringo record. I've played on a Dylan record. And I've played on a George Harrison record. And I'm very, very happy to have had the privilege. ✻

by

PAUL SIMON

"HE WASN'T PARTICULARLY QUIET.

HE *just* DIDN'T DEMAND *to be* HEARD."

THE RAIN HAD LIFTED and the October sun was warm enough for us to pull on pairs of galoshes and stroll across the meadow at Friar Park. An afternoon with George Harrison and his wife, Olivia, was a treat Jeff Kramer (our mutual friend and manager) and I had promised ourselves to relieve the monotony of airplanes, hotel rooms and sound checks–the everyday humdrum of musicians on the road.

I hadn't seen George for several years and was anxious to know, in person, how he was faring after the harrowing attack he'd endured just ten months earlier, on December 30, 1999. "I'm really happy to see you," he said as we shook hands and embraced, "and these days, when I say I'm really happy to see someone, I mean I'm *really* happy."

He looked healthy and his mood was up as we approached a wooden bridge over a pond of waterlilies. I'd never been to Friar Park before, but the rhythm of the wind in the leaves and the cluster chords of autumn's orange, gold and evergreen made it easy to understand why he'd chosen to spend the last thirty years gradually planting, pruning, editing and reshaping the land while at the time recasting himself from pop-culture icon to master gardener.

The three of us paused for a minute at the crest of a hill to let George catch his breath. Gazing down at the black pond, he told us that there were interconnected caves beneath the water's surface, caves that he'd explored before his lung capacity had been diminished by his battle with cancer and a madman's deranged obsession with celebrity. Every gardener knows nature's random cruelty–frost, drought and predators–but most of us are shocked when jagged violence lunges from the shadows and reveals our own vulnerability.

We walked toward the sun and slipped through a copse of weeping willow. There in the middle of a field of wildflowers were two huge boulders weighing several tons and standing one atop the other like a pair of giant granite acrobats. "Are those the work of a sculptor?" I asked. "No," he said, "they came from opposite ends of the property, but we moved them here and stacked them in this field. Everyone wants to know about them. In fact, when Ringo came round for a visit last summer, he asked about them, as well. I told him that Paul's record company had sent them as a promo for his new album, *Standing Stone*. Ringo was really miffed that he hadn't gotten his standing stones, but I said they'd probably only posted them to A-list people." Liverpool accents always sound to me like a joke is coming, but Harrison's wit was deadpan and dead-on.

The roots of my friendship with George Harrison go back to 1976, when we performed together on *Saturday Night Live*. Sitting on stools side by side with acoustic guitars, we sang "Here Comes the Sun" and "Homeward Bound." Though we're in the same generation and weaned on Buddy Holly, Elvis and the Everly Brothers, it must have seemed as strange to him to be harmonizing with someone other than Lennon or McCartney as it was for me to blend with someone other than Art Garfunkel. Nevertheless, it was an effortless collaboration. The mesh of his guitar and voice with my playing and singing gave our duet an ease and musicality that made me realize how intrinsic and subtle his contribution was to the Beatles' brilliant creative weave. He made musicians sound good without calling attention to himself.

His songwriting, too, which I always thought to be stylistically close to mine, was gentle and sad with country and skiffle influences rippling beneath his often sardonic lyrics. It all seemed deceptively simple until masterpieces like "Here Comes the Sun" and "Something" made people realize that the Beatles had three major writers competing for the limited space of the vinyl LP.

They called him "the quiet Beatle," but he wasn't particularly quiet; he simply didn't demand to be heard. He knew who he was, where he'd come from, what he'd accomplished. He wasn't humble, but he projected a humility that implied a vision of his fame seen in a larger context. God gives us color and fragrance, the gardener waters and weeds.

At Friar Park, the rain was threatening an encore, and the English sun sets early at that time of year, so we headed back to the house and the warmth of a fire. Nature's vibrant fall colors are misleading: They imply life and vitality, but they camouflage the muted browns and grays of winter. Soon the leaves will float to the ground and turn to dust, a blanket for a long winter's sleep.

Sitting by the fire, we drank tea and ate chocolate biscuits while George, to my astonishment, played a

miniconcert of Hawaiian music on several ukuleles he'd collected on trips to the islands. His playing was clean and bouncy, his voice sounding like an exact duplicate of George Harrison. I could envision him sitting on a stool side by side with Don Ho, making us wonder how we'd missed the whole Don Ho experience that first time around.

With Simon on 'Saturday Night Live' in November 1976

Before we left, George showed us a copy of the new *Beatles Anthology* book and wrote an inscription to Jeff, deftly adding three perfect forgeries of the other Beatles' signatures.

"Why don't you come down and see the show tonight?" We invited him, knowing there was little chance he'd stir from his chair by the fire. "Maybe we will," he said. "If not, thanks for coming by. I'll see you soon, I hope."

On the drive back to London, Kramer told me that George had felt awkward about not offering a copy of the book to me, but he was afraid I might not have great interest in owning one. I said I'd never asked for anyone's autograph, but I was actually a little disappointed that he hadn't made the offer. Two months later, the tour ended; I came home to find a copy of *The Beatles Anthology* sitting on my desk. "To Paul and Edie," the inscription read, "with lots of love from your pal, George Harrison." ❋

Acknowledgments

*** ❋ * ❋ *** We *** ❋ * ❋ ***

are indebted to many people for making this book as special as it is. We are especially grateful to Olivia and Dhani Harrison for their generous gift of family photos, for Olivia's tender recollections of her husband and for her support. Likewise we thank the many musicians and artists who spoke to us from the direct experience of knowing George and his music. To Jann S. Wenner, perhaps the biggest Beatles fan of us all, who makes loving projects like this possible. The following people provided us with guidance throughout: our publisher David Rosenthal and our editor Bob Bender at Simon & Schuster, as well as Simon & Schuster's Peter McCulloch, Jackie Seow and Johanna Li; and our book agent and all-around book guru Sarah Lazin and her staffers, Paula Balzer and Dena Koklanaris. We literally could not have done this book without our production crew of John Dragonetti, Patrick Cavanaugh, Clifford Cerar, Andrew Cristiano, Gerald Echevarria, DJ Ghezzar, Les Lawrence, Paul Leung, Jack Mittman, Steven Pang, Michael Pirrocco, Vincent Romano, Daniel Shek, Alan Sikiric, Michael Skinner, Richard Waltman and Dennis Wheeler, who handled all the technical magic behind the scenes. We owe many others at ROLLING STONE our thanks, most of whom also worked tirelessly on the ROLLING STONE tribute issue to George Harrison, which provided the blueprints for this book: Will Dana, Tom Nawrocki, Andy Cowles, Nathan Brackett, Peter Travers, Joe Levy, Thomas Walsh, Sarah Pratt, Gaylord Fields, Lauren Goldstein, Fiona McDonagh, Mark Binelli, Matt Diehl, Ruthie Epstein, Coco McPherson, Allison Miller, Urania Mylonas, Evan Schlansky, Ashley Parish, Darren Ratner, Corey Sabourin, Joy M. Sanchez, Nate Schweber, Rob Sheffield, Sarah Wilson, Sean Woods, Stephanie Delk, Teri Tsang, Maureen Lamberti and Elizabeth Gorzelany. We are also grateful for the efforts of Gavin de Becker, Elizabeth Freund and Ambrosia Healy, and for the guiding spirit of Holly George-Warren. And we thank those who helped us with the art that is the cornerstone of the book: Jorge Jaramillo at AP Photo, Danny Bennett, Chris Murray and Govinda Gallery, David Plotkin at Corbis, Michael Rowe at Corbis Outline, Barry Feinstein, Florence Nash at Gamma Press, Colleen Stoll at Getty Images, William Stuart at London Features, Malli Kamimura at Magnum Photos, Jim and Cynthia Keltner, Mike and Brian at Patient Pictures, Neal Preston, John E. Espinosa at Retna Ltd., Chuck Musse at Rex Features, Carl Studna, Virginia Lohle at Starfile and Kathy Hopkins at Timepix. Finally, thank you to George Harrison for the way your music and your life have touched us all. ~JASON FINE

Contributors

ANDY BABIUK
is the author of *Beatles Gear,* a guide to the group's instruments and equipment. He works at House of Guitars in Rochester, New York, and is a consultant for the Rock and Roll Hall of Fame.

* * *

ADAM DAWTREY
is *Variety* magazine's European editor.

* * *

ANTHONY DECURTIS
is a ROLLING STONE contributing editor and the author of a recent collection of essays, *Rocking My Life Away.* He is a Grammy Award–winning writer, and the host of "The A List with Anthony DeCurtis," on GetMusic.com.

* * *

JENNY ELISCU
is an assistant editor at ROLLING STONE.

* * *

JASON FINE
is a senior editor at ROLLING STONE, where he has worked since 1997.

BEN FONG-TORRES
began writing for ROLLING STONE in 1968 and served as a senior editor until 1981. His books include *Not Fade Away, The Motown Album, Hickory Wind, The Rice Room* and the recently reissued *The Hits Just Keep On Coming.*

* * *

DAVID FRICKE
has been writing for ROLLING STONE since the late Seventies; currently he is a senior editor, and has been on staff since 1985. He is a two-time winner of the ASCAP-Deems Taylor Award and has written liner notes for CD reissues by the Byrds, the Ramones, Moby Grape and the Velvet Underground.

* * *

MIKAL GILMORE
is a ROLLING STONE contributing editor and has been writing for the magazine since 1976. He is also the author of *Night Beat: A Shadow History of Rock & Roll* and the autobiographical *Shot in the Heart,* recently adapted to film for HBO.

NICK JONES
was ROLLING STONE's "London correspondent" in the late Sixties, when he was still in his teens.

* * *

GREG KOT
is the pop music critic for the *Chicago Tribune* and a frequent contributor to ROLLING STONE. He has also contributed to *Encyclopædia Britannica* and *The Trouser Press Guide to '90s Rock.*

* * *

ROBERT LOVE
is ROLLING STONE's managing editor. He has been on staff at the magazine since 1982.

* * *

AUSTIN SCAGGS
is ROLLING STONE's Random Notes editor.

* * *

CHARLES M. YOUNG
is a former editor at ROLLING STONE and frequent contributor to the magazine. His writing also appears in *Playboy* and *Men's Journal.*

Photography Credits

"

THERE
NEVER WAS A TIME
WHEN YOU NOR I
NOR ALL THESE KINGS
DID NOT EXIST,
NOR WILL THERE BE
ANY FUTURE WHEN WE
CEASE TO BE.

"

— A FAVORITE QUOTE *of* GEORGE HARRISON'S
from the Bhagavad Gita